Hanna's Story

Perseverance and Love Escaping Nazi Germany and Homesteading Wyoming

Hanna Bodle

Story Capture by Marilyn C. Bodle and Janet A. Gregory

Printed by CreateSpace Independent Publishing
North Charleston, SC

www.createspace.com

ISBN-13: 978-1727102796
ISBN-10: 1727102797

CreateSpace Independent Publishing Platform
North Charleston, South Carolina

Dedicated to
my beloved Marvin.

For
my children, grandchildren, great-grandchildren
and beyond.

Connecting family history of the past
to family history of the future
which has yet to be written.

Acknowledgements

For a rich wealth of family experience:

Marilyn Bodle, co-authoring, stories, photos, and editing
Selma Watkins, stories, and photos
Allen Bodle, stories
Bud Bodle, stories
Robbin Bodle, stories

For generous assistance in manuscript review:

- Janet Gregory, co-authoring, cover, writing, and editing
- Judy & Marle Hewett, content, copy, and line editing
- Chloe Fitzmyers, photo editing
- Marilyn Harnish, peer review

- Linda Fabian
  Wyoming State historical Society
- Jeremy M. Johnston, Ph.D.
  Curator of the Buffalo Bill Museum
- Phil Roberts, J.D., Ph.D.
  Professor of History Emeritus, University of Wyoming

Life is a Work in Progress
First biography draft 2013 by Janet Gregory
Published article in Pine Mountain Lake News, June 2013
Second & third biography drafts in 2016 copied for family reunion

First autobiographical draft 2017 by Marilyn Bodle
Second autobiographical draft 2018 edited by Janet Gregory
Autobiography published as public version & private family edition

Table of Contents

Preface

There are so many amazing and interesting people who cross our path in life. Some we see, some we don't.

Just seven years ago I moved into a wonderful community and started meeting my neighbors. People came here from all walks of life, diverse careers, different backgrounds, mixed education, and wide-ranging interests. Most speak only of who they are today and where their life is heading. With a few well-positioned questions, I unfastened rich histories, mostly unspoken. One such story belongs to Hanna Bodle.

The people I meet fascinate me. I began writing their stories in short articles for our local monthly newspaper. It's hard to capture a lifetime of experience in 500 words, about 4-5 minutes if spoken aloud. But, I tried. And, I loved it. The people I met were a treasure. Conquerors, adventurers, heroes, travelers, and more. All had a wisdom, understanding, and insight beyond the ordinary. Hertha Hanna Kranz Bodle is one of the extraordinary people that I met. Humble, cheerful, unpretentious, and in my mind, a sort of citizen hero.

In my first interview with Hanna, we spent about two hours in conversation. It was enough for a short article but wasn't there more? Had she written down her story? No. It existed only as a series of short oral tales recounted at gatherings of family or friends. I wanted more. Her story deserved more. We met several more times and the short article blossomed into a biography.

Hanna and I met at her California home of more than fifty years. Her daughter Marilyn joined me in the journey and together, the three of us, transformed the biography back into Hanna's own words.

This is Hanna's memoir. It is not a history lesson, but it is an accurate account of Hanna's experience. It's a chronology of her life, but not every little detail. As a memoir it captures her early years growing up in Germany and building a life for herself in America, which shaped her.

We think that today's world is complicated – and it is. But, our struggles in America are minor as compared with those involved in war or building a life from nothing. Today people often think that they are "owed" or "entitled" to something. Through Hanna I learned that life is what you make it, how you stand up to it, and what possibilities you create for yourself.

I think of Hanna as a citizen hero. She fully participates in her community, giving of herself and standing up for what she believes in; she is a good citizen. Hanna has conquered difficulties. She sees beyond the challenge, finding possibilities. She is not Superman or Superwoman, but she is a shining star, a quiet leader, with great inner strength.

I am honored that Hanna gave me the opportunity to assist in capturing her story. I hope you enjoy the journey as much as I have.

Janet A. Gregory

Hanna's Story

Perseverance and Love Escaping Nazi Germany and Homesteading Wyoming

My Story

There are things that happen in our lives that mark time for us. For me, the first mile marker was the war, World War II. I would talk about things as "before the war" or "after the war". It left such a dramatic impression on me that everything else was in reference to it. I don't know if I am any different than anyone else but I had several mile markers in my life. Some were very happy like marrying Marvin, having children, and connecting with my family. Others were very difficult, like the war, the prairie fire, and losing people I love.

Throughout life I have tried to stand tall in both good times and bad. I think it's a funny thing to say, since I am only 4'10" tall, and maybe even a little shorter now. I lived my life and I lived it the best I could, standing tall on my principles and my faith. My name is Hertha Hanna Kranz Bodle but most people know me as Hanna Bodle. This is my story.

Jaentsdorf

My story starts a long, long time ago in a faraway land. Really. I'm in my 90s now; so that's a long time ago. I was born half way around the world.

My tiny village of Jaentsdorf was located in the province of Schlesien, a region in the eastern part of Germany. If you were looking for it on the maps today, you wouldn't find it. This area was annexed to Poland in 1945. I don't remember it happening but know that it did. It was a political thing.

Jaentsdorf dates back to before the time of the black plague in Europe, before 1350 in the fourteenth century. Our small family farm had been on my mother's side of the family since before that time. There were about two dozen homes and shops along the one main road that ran through the center of the village. The lower part of the dorf (or village) was home to about half the people, including a blacksmith shop and the mill. A large lake and a couple of smaller ponds surrounded the village, along with creeks that connected them and ran through the village. The upper part of the dorf

2

had the rest of the people, a butcher shop, the church, and a guest house with a huge Linden tree where guests could tie up their horses in the shade.

Our church was across the street from the guest house and the graveyard. The church had a foot-pedal powered organ, called a pump organ or harmonium. This smaller organ was less expensive than a larger pipe organ. Our little community could not afford a big pipe organ, and our church was too small for one anyway. Just up from the guest house was the mercantile or small market. Scattered between were homes of the villagers. Our home was near the church and guest house. Our home was on the family farm which had passed down to the oldest child of each family before my mother.

Entering the village from the lower part, we came through a beautiful estate. The estate belonged to the land baron, the Von Powley family, who was some sort of royalty. They raised cattle and sheep along with sugar beets, potatoes, and other crops, as well as Flax (for linen cloth). Some cows were raised for meat and others for milk; they had a big creamery on the estate that shipped a lot of milk into the city. They hired Polish youth to work in the fields during the summer months and the fall. The Von Powley family had lots of beautiful carriages and buggies; they were the very first people to get a car. For the most part they were very friendly people, especially Mrs. Von Powley, who always shared with the village folks.

Speaking of cars, there was great excitement when the very first truck came to town; it cut the delivery time for getting milk to the rail station in half. The other village men would offer to pay the truck owner to carry their milk into town. We only had three telephones in town: one at the land baron's home, one at the guest house, and one at the post office. The one at the post office was a public phone for the village folks to use. *How things have changed; today we carry a phone in our purse or pocket!*

A creek ran through the back of the village into several small ponds and then into a larger pond before becoming a stream. The water was so clean you could see the trout swimming in it. The first pond was a small diverted pond near the blacksmith shop. It was mainly used for the horses. Now and then they would let us kids swim in it. The next pond was also a small diversion pond for the mill. Once a month the mill owner would place planks of wood in the pond as a temporary dam allowing the water to build up into a much larger lake. Everyone who had grain, or whatever they needed to mill, would bring it to the mill to be ground on the old stone wheels that were turned by the water. Afterwards the planks were removed and water would once more be allowed to flow freely. This pond was where the bony carp lived; no one really liked eating them but some people did. It was a lovely place to ice skate in winter, swim in summer, or just hang out.

Our school house was up on a hill near the creek. The school house had a small garden and beyond it rolled a beautiful little meadow. We would play in the meadow during recess. I loved to play! We could turn anything into fun, an old sack, a rope, or pebbles. We would have gunnysack races, jump rope, or play games with pebbles and sticks. It was a one-room school house that served all grades from first through eighth. The building was pretty dark inside making it hard to read but somehow, we managed. The school master and his wife did all the teaching and lessons. He was very strict. If you did something wrong, you got punished on the spot, out came the switch or the ruler, with no mercy. Boys had to reach over, touch their ankles, and they got swatted. Girls got rapped on the hand. Sometimes one of the kids had to sit on a stool with a large cone-shaped hat on his or her head for all the rest of the class to look at.

The school master taught the boys football (soccer) and other sports, and they would play against neighboring villages. The school master's wife was a sweet lady. During the warmer days with the longer light she would take us girls to her summer house to learn sewing, knitting, or embroidery. In the fall we would be allowed to pick apples. She taught us how to tell when they were ripe and ready to pick. If we picked an apple, we had to eat it right there; food was not to be wasted. Sometimes she would bring a beautiful apple dessert to school for all of us to enjoy, especially if we helped her pick the apples that were up high in the tree.

One day the giant Linden tree in the village split. I don't know why it split; it may have been lightning. The people of the village gathered to discuss the fate of this beautiful tree. No one really wanted to see the tree come down; as far as everyone knew the tree had been there forever. My father, several other men, and the blacksmith decided they wanted to save the tree. They made a huge metal band to ring the tree at the break, so that it could heal. I was told that it worked and that the tree was still standing twenty years ago.

My Life Begins

My great-grandparents, on my mother's side, were Heinrich Vetter and Christione (Schuster) Vetter. They had a daughter Emmilie (also called Emilia), who was my grandmother. They lived in an old stone house that had been passed down in the family through many generations. This house became my Grandmother Emilia's home. Records show that Grandmother Emilia was born October 22, 1850 and died March 10, 1939, at age 89.

My grandfather, Wilhelm Wahler, was the son of Karl Wahler and Karoline (Rodewald) Wahler. Records show that Grandfather Wilhelm was born February 14, 1855 and died nine years before Grandmother Emilia on June 10, 1930, at age 75.

Emilia and Wilhelm Wahler had two daughters: Emma (born September 19, 1895) and Selma (born August 3, 1901).

That old stone house had withstood time. The ivy that grew on the outside was so thick that it had to be chopped away each year to allow the storm shutters to close in bad weather. It was like that ivy held the old house together. The house dated back to the 1800s and had been built to replace other houses that stood on the same spot. The old stone house was dark inside and had a special smell that was unique. The smell was a pleasant musty mix of age, grandpa's pipe tobacco, and whatever grandma was cooking. I loved going there and listening to grandma read from the Bible by the light of an oil lamp; grandpa sat beside her nodding and puffing on his pipe, occasionally discussing the meaning of the words.

The old stone house was a simple one-room building divided into three sections. On one side of the house was the kitchen with a door that went out to a small covered porch and artesian well. A large fireplace dominated the center of the house and on the backside was an old wood stove that grandma cooked on. They had no sink; dishes were done in a large pan. A small table and chairs for dining, working, and talking stood along the wall next to the kitchen cupboard. On the other side of the room, beyond the fireplace that stood in the middle, was a curtain that could be drawn during the day to cover their tiny little bed and an old chest that housed what few clothes they had. A few feet from the house was the outhouse.

It was a simple building that faithfully served many generations. I often wonder how they managed to raise two girls in that tiny little house. Forever etched in my memory is that old stone house sitting there in its glory, the thatched roof, ivy clinging to its stone walls, and the soft trickle of the artesian well as it spilled into the trough freely flowing to the pond below. *Many years later, I heard that the Pollocks, who had gotten the place, tore down that beautiful old stone house looking for hidden treasures. There were none, except for treasured family memories. Now there is only stone rubble with artesian water flowing through it. It's sad.*

Grandpa Wahler was a skilled craftsman in the carpenter trade, making beautiful doors and cabinets. Grandpa Wahler was taught the trade by his father (my great-grandfather), and there were stories of many beautiful doors that he made for the churches and cathedrals, fulfilling commissions as far away as Spain.

My grandfather, on my father's side, Gottlieb Kranz, was a skilled craftsman in the blacksmith trade. He did ornamental iron work including hinges and knobs that hung large doors and shutters. Like Grandpa Wahler, Grandpa Kranz learned the trade from his father. My two great-grandfathers did work for some of the same churches and cathedrals. Like father, like son, they became close friends and often exchanged work between the two of them. They did not live in the same town, but stayed close just the same.

Grandpa Gottlieb Kranz and his wife Pauline Neldner Kranz had eight children, three boys and five girls. The youngest children were twins, a boy and a girl.

The story goes, that one-day (grandpa) Gottlieb Kranz wrote to ask if his son could do some apprentice work under (grandpa) Wilhelm Wahler. His son, Karl, was already highly skilled with iron work and showed great promise with wood. He was a strong lad and could do most anything. Karl had served in World War I and was now in need of a trade.

Wilhelm agreed to take Karl Kranz in as an apprentice. Karl moved to Jaentsdorf to study under (grandpa) Wilhelm Wahler's skillful knowledge of the carpentry business.

This is how my parents met. My father, Karl Kranz, worked in grandpa's carpentry shop, learning the trade, and helping with the farming chores. As part of his keep, he was allowed to stay in a small room just off the carpentry shop.

My mother, Selma, was a governess and would watch the children of the wealthier families in town when they needed help or went away. She was sought after by many families because of her gentle ways and polite manner. She loved the garden and the healing ways of nature. This was what my father loved so much about my mom. Selma and Karl were a wonderful pair. Selma was often quite serious and Karl could be quite funny. She might be madder than a hornet at him but he would wiggle those big ears, smile, and she would melt.

During the time of Karl's apprenticeship Grandpa Wahler started to build a larger brick house close to the road for grandma and him. Karl helped him build the new house as part of the apprenticeship.

Grandpa Wahler liked the way young Karl worked and was pleased to see his daughter taken by him, as was Grandpa Kranz. On the other hand, Grandma Pauline Kranz wanted nothing to do with this and did not want to hear talk of them getting married. She was a strong Catholic and insisted that Karl must marry a Catholic girl. The Wahlers were Evangelists. Love and nature can change things, even back in those days. It took some time, but after seven years of being together, Karl and Selma were finally married with everyone's blessing.

The Wahler family was happy with their new son. Even Grandpa Kranz was pleased, but sadly, Grandma Kranz remained angry. She would never come to see us and was not particularly friendly when papa took us to visit her. As a result, papa didn't take us to visit her very often.

The day my parents were married, my sweet and beloved grandparents turned the new brick house over to them. It was in this brick house built by my grandpa and Karl that life would begin for me, then later my brothers and sisters.

I was born, Herta Hanna Kranz on Wednesday, March 29th, 1926 in that brick house. Everyone called me Herta.

Papa's skills improved and expanded. He was called to do many different things. At this time, we made nearly everything ourselves. Papa could make furniture and doors, he could do fancy iron work, and his love for the land and animals was great.

Papa liked to whittle. He would sit with the other men, whittling and talking for hours. I don't know what they talked about; it seemed like everything and nothing all at the same time. He whittled all kinds of things from wood. He made his own pipes. He would also whittle things for the kids in the village, like whistles. They each had their own different sound. He told me, "Whenever you hear this sound, you come running." So, when I heard papa blowing that whistle, I knew it was time to get right home from Grandma's, the pond, or playing, and not waste any time.

When I was about seven years old, papa traveled to America with another man who was an inventor of some type of machinery. They went to the Chicago World's Fair. This was very exciting for papa because it was all about progress and innovation, with the motto "Science finds, industry applies, man adapts." Papa told us wondrous stories about America: the vast open spaces, the magic of the World Fair, and how people from all over the world came to see it. Papa was gone over a month because it took nearly two weeks to cross the ocean by ship.

My mother was a quiet and gentle lady. She had long hair that she would braid to fashion into a bun or wrap around her head. I thought she was the most beautiful woman I had ever seen when she was brushing her hair. Her hair was dark, like mine. She loved being in the garden and among the animals. She seemed to know everything about the plants, including what they could do to make you feel better. When she cooked the house smelled like heaven. In my little eyes, mom could do everything! She kept everything running smoothly. Every day had a set of things to be done and she always got them done. As the family grew, I was amazed at how she could keep up. The house was always warm and welcoming, usually set with a small bouquet of flowers from the garden or with a bowl of fruit from the orchards.

Once a week a large outdoor oven would be fired up. It took a lot of wood and a lot of time to fire up this big oven, so the women shared the work. They would fire up an oven at one of the homes, bring over their baked goods to cook, then share amongst the families. The large oven would stay hot for a several days, so nearly everyone got to have fresh baked bread and rolls. I loved baking day; the whole village would smell so yummy.

We raised everything we ate, or nearly everything. We didn't grow oranges, I don't know where they came from but when we had them, it was the ultimate treat. We ate meat only on Wednesday and Sunday. The rest of the week's meals were vegetable dishes, eggs, or what little was left over if any. We raised chickens, geese, pigs, sheep, rabbits, bees, and a cow. We also had a horse. There was always a dog and cat or two. The farm was about 20 acres. We also grew sugar beets, some grains, potatoes, cabbage, and root crops like carrots, parsnips, and turnips. There were berries of different sorts too. In the orchard were apple, cherry, pear, peach, and plum trees, along with walnuts and hazelnuts.

One of the saddest days of my young life, was when grandpa Wahler passed away. I was only four and didn't understand about life and death. I couldn't grasp what had happened. Why did he leave me? I want to play with him.

Everyone told me that Grandpa had gone to heaven to be with Jesus. I just couldn't understand. Why had he left me and Grandma behind?

A group of us were taught to sing by a man from the church. I am not sure that I would call it a choir but we would sing on Sundays and at special occasions. Our group was all ages and sizes but mostly kids. Whenever there was a funeral, we would get all cleaned up, dressed in our Sunday best, and sing at the church services and at the grave. Gerda had a beautiful deep voice. As for me, I was not very good.

Figure 1: Me with Grandma Emilia, 1934

A few years later Grandma Emilia came to live in the big brick house with us. She took me to church and taught me about God's way. We loved to sing songs in church, along with the rest of the community. Even if we were off key or off beat, it didn't matter, as long as we were together. It broke my heart when we lost Grandma Emilia. She went to heaven to be with Grandpa Whaler and Jesus when I was thirteen, about nine years after Grandpa left us. Grandma Emilia was such an important part of my growing up. As she got older, one of my responsibilities was to take care of things that were difficult for her to do herself. I loved helping her and being with her.

Now as I look back on this time, I regret that I had not done a better job of listening to my grandparent's stories and advice. If only I had a crystal ball and knew what was to lay ahead of me, I would have done things differently. I would have spent more time learning the lessons they tried to teach me. I would have paid more attention to mother's descriptions of how each plant could heal or flavor a meal. I would have listened more intently when papa talked about the different types of wood and how to fix something. I would have tried harder to hone my skills with plants and herbs. I would have learned to make things from scratch, like soap, or how to cure and preserve foods. I did learn to sew and darn, even a little embroidery. But sadly, my cooking skills were not very good when I left home, so I missed out on learning to make strudel and noodles.

You can't go back and redo what has been done. No one knows what lays ahead. My advice to you is to live each and every day with no regrets. Listen carefully to your elders. Try to walk away with some of their knowledge and show them respect and love for who they are and what they have done in life. Slow down and play in the soil like a child. Marvel at the wonders of the earth and do your best to help protect her.

All Four Seasons

Spring was, and is, my favorite time of year. I love spring because of the all the new life that comes with it. In spring we would help get the gardens and fields ready. Mother had me help her in the green house growing little starters. I loved everything about spring — the sound of new baby animals everywhere; the smell of a new puppy or kitten; the softness of a new lamb, pony, or calf; the adorable face of a piglet; and the sight of little tiny chicks or goslings following their mommy.

In the spring we had a custom where the kids would wear the traditional garment for the area. The girls wore green and white dirndls with a little apron. The boys wore pants similar to lederhosen. We would make beautiful colored sticks decorated with paper, cloth or whatever was available. With decorated sticks in hand, we would gather into small groups, going from homes to shops singing songs of spring. Sometimes we would get a special treat of cookies or candy. If we were really fortunate, we might get one of those treasured oranges; then we would sing an extra song or two! As May approached, we would join a much larger celebration for the spring planting and blessing for a promising harvest. For this celebration our parents and the elders would join us with lots of food and music. A large pole would be raised in the village square; there would be long colored ribbons tied to the top of the pole with a large ring. We would dance and weave the ribbon around that pole, making it quite beautiful. The decorated pole would stay standing for a while, then it disappeared. It was so much fun because we were allowed to stay up a little later at night and play with our friends.

Summer wasn't really my favorite time of year. When school was out, we had to help our parents with work on the farm or in the house. We would work in the fields, orchards, and gardens, or help tend the little kids so mother could do the heavier work. As I got older, I was given more responsibilities even though I was so small. I often helped take care of the younger children or Grandma Wahler, especially after grandpa passed away. I helped mother more in the garden and with the livestock than in the fields.

My sister, Gerda, was bigger and stronger, so she would help papa in the fields.

Most afternoons we would be allowed a couple of hours to play with our friends. One summer day we had gotten into trouble for something and were not allowed to go swimming with the other kids. As we watched the other kids having fun and could not join in, one of us came up with a brilliant idea. We had a very large and overly loving Saint Bernard named Berny. Berny was more than just a dog: he was smart and was always on our side. We decided to send Berny down to get our friends out of the water. He was determined to get every one of those boys and girls out of the pond and he did! We hid in the bushes watching and laughing, until we got laughing so hard that we stood up and got caught. Most summer evenings were spent chasing fireflies as the elders sat and talked.

I liked fall because of the change in the air and the colors that it brought. It was the busiest time of year in our village as everyone was preparing for the oncoming winter. I was always very busy with both school and harvest. There was lots of work in the kitchen canning vegetables and fruits to be put away into the root cellar. Mother made sauerkraut and dried fruit too.

In the nearby forest, trees would be marked for thinning and people could buy them. This was important for many reasons. Papa would buy some fire wood and others were selected for making cabinets and furniture. The forest was some distance from the village, about 12 miles. When trees were cut and ready to haul back to the village, they would to be dragged behind a horse or two. This would keep the men busy for days. Papa came up with an idea to make this chore easier; with the help of a fellow villager, they built a skid. The skid was in two parts connected in the middle with a chain or rope. They discovered they could haul very long poles and up to five at a time. The skid made it easier to navigate corners and they could get the whole job done in less time. The village celebrated his new invention.

As October drew to a close, it was time for a big community celebration. A large crown made of wheat straw was placed on a big wooden plank and adorned with the various crops we had raised, everything from fruits to vegetables, to nuts. The kids that worked in the fields and gardens during spring and summer were each given a crown with their name on it. We carried the plank from place to place in the village. When we came to the church we carried it inside to be blessed by the pastor. There was lots of singing and dancing, games and food. Everyone came out and lined the streets. It was a joyous time, the best time of the year for me, as it will always be. All the villages and towns celebrated the harvest, each in their own way.

Then came the cold and snow as old man winter set in. It was time for the land to rest and life could slow down a bit. Just before Christmas we would butcher the young goslings for market, saving all the soft down feathers to work on in the winter. When I was a child, this was a beloved season. It was a time when we mostly stayed indoors helping mother or grandma. It was time to practice our sewing skills under mother's watchful eye, read a book, or make crafts. It was a time for sharing when we would start thinking of Old Saint Nicolas and what we could make as Christmas gifts for family or friends. It was also the time when we removed all the quills from those down feathers to make more feather bedding with mother. There was always a need for another blanket or pillow as new members were born into the family or as the old bedding got lumpy. It was a time when we ate all that wonderful food that mother and grandma had canned and carefully stored away in those special glass jars with rubber rings and wire clips. In winter we ate lots of stews and homemade noodle dishes. Even though things slowed down a bit, we were still busy. We had to walk to school, do our school work, and come home to do our chores. When the road flooded and we couldn't cross the road to get to school, we thought it was a special day. But then we had to work even harder at school to make up the lessons we missed.

One Christmas, when I was about four years old, Grandpa Wahler made a rocker for my sister and me. It was in the shape of a beautiful swan and was hand painted. We would sit down inside on a small bench seat, grab the handle between its head, and rock back and forth endlessly. Gerda was about eighteen months old at the time. It really didn't fit both of us at the same time so Grandpa would make us girls take turns. That beautiful rocker was still there when I left home and went away to school; it was being used by the younger kids.

Christmas was a special time. Typical at this time of year, papa was working late in the shop and we were NOT allowed to go in. We could take him meals on a little table, bringing it into the small room where he lived during his apprenticeship, and yelling for him that it was time to come eat. Somehow mother always seemed to keep us kids from being too curious about what he was doing. As you can imagine, he was often working on gifts for us, the family, or others and didn't want the secret let outside of the shop.

As winter came in with shorter days, more snow, and the nights grew darker, we were kept in the house most of the time. In the evening papa would go out to check on the livestock or check the stove in his workshop to make sure he hadn't left the glue pot on it. Sometimes he would be gone for hours. Mother would finish cleaning us up and getting us off to bed.

On Christmas Eve we would walk into the woods to pick out a tree to cut down and bring home. We dragged that tree home singing songs and laughing. A few snow balls went flying at each other too. Mother had hot milk and cookies ready when we arrived home with rosy red cheeks and cold noses. Papa set up the tree. We made decorations of

16

colorful paper and mother would gently place candles on the tree. It was magical. Christmas Eve night we would sit beside that beautiful tree and sing more songs. Mother and papa told us the story of Christmas and about the birth of Christ. I have wonderful memories of the fire dancing in the fire place and snowflakes falling outside. After supper we put on our jackets, were given a candle, and walked across the street to the church for Christmas service. It was so special.

Christmas morning the house was filled with excitement. We raced from our beds to see if Saint Nicolas had been able to stop by the house. With sweet joy, we would find an orange tucked in the toe of our stocking, a handful of hard candy, a whistle, or some other small carved toy.

One Christmas season when I was twelve or thirteen, papa had been secretly working on a project for several months. After breakfast on Christmas morning, we went out to do our chores, as usual. We were not the only ones that needed to be fed; we had to feed the animals. In addition to the dogs and livestock, we had two horses, their names were Hans and Gretchen. Hans was a large horse and very gentle; he would always lower his head for me. Gretchen was another story. She was not very cooperative. Gretchen would do what Gerda wanted, but not me. I guess that's where Gerda's larger size was a real asset. In addition to feeding them, it was our job to keep the horse stalls clean. I always chose to feed and clean Hans, maybe because I wasn't afraid of him.

As we finished feeding the animals that Christmas morning, I could hear papa in the shop and mother shout, "Oh my God, it's beautiful!" We heard all of this, but wondered if we should dare to look in after being banned from his shop for months. Then papa whistled for us. I scooped up all the kids and we ran to see what was going on. There in the shop stood the most beautiful sleigh I have ever seen. Next to it was a brand-new harness set out for Hans. The harness

17

was smooth polished leather with bells on it. The snow was just begging for a sleigh ride. Hans was so proud of his new harness and bells that tinkled as he trotted along. We nearly wore poor Hans out that day! As the time passed, I learned to drive the sleigh with Hans pulling it. We would make deliveries into other villages for my mother. Hans and I did that together for several years until I left for high school in Breslau.

The War

When I was about fourteen, I was sent to the city to attend a trade school and finish my higher education. This was arranged by my parents along with my aunt and uncle who lived in the city of Breslau (Now Wroclaw, Poland). There were no high schools in our area, so to advance beyond eight grade I would have to leave for the big city. Eighth grade was the highest level that our little one-room school taught. Those of us, who were lucky enough to have relatives or friends that lived in the city and would take us in, would leave home to attend high school or beyond. Of course, this came with a big price tag, much like sending kids off to college today.

My Aunt Louise (Grandma Whaler's sister) and Uncle Paul lived near the train station in Breslau. This was very convenient for Uncle Paul who worked for the railroad and for me when I would stay with them. My aunt and uncle rented out their extra bedroom to another lady. I slept in a small bed placed in the entrance hall. In exchange for my room and board, mother sent fresh produce, eggs, butter, and fruit with me each Sunday when I returned to Breslau from home.

Each Sunday afternoon I rode my bicycle with three others to the train station in the next village. We left our bikes chained at the station until the following weekend, costing us twenty-five cents a week. We took the train into the city where we spent the week at school and studying. It was a routine that we did every week.

People in the city dressed differently than we did. They wore different shoes and clothing. They looked down on the country people. Some of the people had "high noses", yet others seemed to be interested in country life. My aunt came to my rescue right away sewing several dresses, more suited for city life. I soon fit in, feeling comfortable in the city, and had several friends. My friend Elizabeth came home with me several times. Elizabeth loved animals but as a city girl didn't have any, so when she came home with me she had a ball. She learned to cluck like a chicken and crow like the rooster; it was the funniest thing! Darn, if Elizabeth wouldn't do that every chance she got.

The lady that rented a room from my aunt and uncle taught me about taking care of my skin and different hygiene practices. She taught at the college. I follow her practices to this day. "Wash your face at bedtime and always brush your teeth", she would say.

The city of Breslau was big, especially compared to Jaentsdorf, which was a small village. It's like comparing Sacramento to Groveland in California. Breslau had a brand-new shopping center. It was a huge building with several floors, filled with all sorts of different items. The most exciting thing about this shopping center was the <u>moving stairs</u> or escalator. It was unbelievable. Who would have ever thought to create such a thing? It was so much fun to go there and ride those moving stairs to the different floors.

Years later, a half a world away and a half a lifetime away, I was working for a company called Becton-Dickinson in Los Gatos, California where I met Dr. Barasch. As we got talking and got to know more about one another, we realized that we both lived in Breslau at the same time. In one conversation I mentioned those remarkable moving stairs.

To my total amazement he told me that it was his family, the Barasch family that owned the shopping center with the moving stairs! Dr. Barasch's family was Jewish. He and his family spent time in a German concentration camp. He was able to keep his mother and sibling alive by playing the piano for his Nazi captors.

While in Breslau I took several courses studying to be a nurse. I also took English classes. I was going into my third year of schooling when the war broke out. It was in the midst of my precious teenage years; all my dreams and ideas for the future were taken away in one swift blow. Like most able-bodied people, I was pressed into service by the German military. Maybe it could be called being drafted or conscription, but the truth is that **we were just told what to do**. The friends that I rode the train to school with were now being drafted and sent away. My boyfriend was also drafted and sent away. *(Later I learned of his ill fate.)* I had just turned seventeen when I was drafted. I was taken to a training facility in Brig, in the far eastern part of the Schlesien region. *I would never see my aunt and uncle again or any of my school friends.*

Life began to show me a very different side. We were loaded onto train cars and taken to a small training camp with cold unheated barracks and no hot water. We were woken up early every morning to do military training. We were divided up into small groups and each group had a barrack commander. We had to make our beds just right; if the bed clothes were not tight enough, the bed was torn apart and we had to make it again. Clothes had to be hung just so or the barrack commander would throw everything on the floor and we would have to start all over. We were only given a short amount of time to do all of this. After these morning rituals there was school or specialized training. Each of us was selected for our strengths. Some girls were trained in office skills while others, like me, were trained to help care for the sick and wounded.

Many friendships were forged during those difficult and stressful times. We shared barracks and bunks. We worked together, ate together, and slept in the same cramped space. All of us young girls were trying to cope with life. *A lifetime of experience was wrapped into two intense months of work. Here is where my life really changed forever.*

I have always made friends easily and this time in my life was no different. I became very close with the girls in my barrack, especially two of them, Sofie and Vera. These friendships proved to be the best thing to happen from that time.

Figure 2: My barracks at Nurses Training, 1940

Sofie gave me the nickname of Schnucki (pronounced snookie). Sofie was from Austria. Our friendship grew deep and still remains strong to this day. Sofie was trained in office skills, did a lot of record keeping, and that sort of stuff. We often got into trouble because of her pranks, but they were mostly harmless. Her mother wanted me to make sure she went to confession, which she did, but only for her mother's sake.

After the war, Sofie married a British pilot who was wounded; they moved to Birmingham, England and had three exceptional children.

Vera was German, from Wolfenbuttel in the northern part of the country. She was beautiful. She had striking red hair and fair skin. The three of us, Sofie, Vera, and me, were always up to something. It's curious that even in times of war, you can still find things to laugh about.

The last time I saw Vera, she was living in Bremen, Germany. She married a Frenchman after the war but it turned out to be a bad deal. She told me, "The only good thing that came out of that marriage was my beautiful daughter and granddaughter." She moved to Munich to be near her daughter and that was the last I heard from her. I often wonder what became of her after that.

Figure 3: Sofie, Vera, and me (in back) at Training Camp, 1940

We shared good times and bad times during those short months of training.

Occasionally we put on little plays for the village folks; that was fun. Once when we had done something wrong, we had to clean all the chimneys of the barracks which was a dirty and nasty job. Sofie still made it fun.

One day at training camp I was called away to help deliver a baby. The only doctor in town was an older gentleman who had eye sight problems. My commander ordered me to go and assist with the delivery. This was something I had never done before. There was no hospital or real supplies on hand and the poor woman was having a difficult labor. I was still there long after curfew. Sofie somehow convinced the camp leader to allow her to come check on me, and bring me back to camp. It was beginning to get dark so Sofie brought along another girl. When they arrived, the baby still had not come yet. They had to return to camp without me. On the way back they met some soldiers, got to talking, got back to camp way after dark, and got into a lot of trouble. As for me, that baby boy came into this world wet and hollering in the early hours of the morning. I was thankful for the helpful instruction of the old blind doctor. It was really very gratifying to bring a new life into this world. On my return to the training camp, I reported the late arrival of the baby which in return helped save Sofie and the other girl from being reprimanded.

Not far from our camp was a training camp for young men being trained to be pilots. Sometimes when they flew over they would drop little notes to us from the air. A few times we were allowed to go dancing with these soldiers, but it was always under the watchful eye of our camp leader. Sofie later told me that a couple of girls would sneak out to meet with the soldiers and ended up getting pregnant.

War makes a person stronger. While in training camp there were not enough nurses and not enough could be trained to fill the need. Rail cars were beginning to pour in with wounded and dying men from the front lines. Like many

24

others, I was drafted before my training was completed. It was now a hands-on approach to learning. My first position was in an Army Hospital. Because of my young age, I worked with (or maybe for) the Red Cross. My first job was learning to feed and clean wounded soldiers. I relieved the overworked trained nurses giving them some much-needed rest. It was busy and non-stop. It was hard work and very gruesome at times. I had never seen such horrible things before, and at first, it actually left me feeling sick to my stomach. I don't know if you can imagine the sight of bandages oozing with blood, badly burned bodies, or someone who lost a leg or arm. The moaning and crying from the pain broke my heart; there was little we could really do for them. It left me shaking yet it gave me strength to be humble and kind, trying to do whatever I could to help them.

As the war continued, I was transferred into the field to help bring the wounded in from the front lines.

War is a very, very ugly thing. There is no glamor. There are no winners. Everyone loses something in war.

My Battle Wound

I carry a scar on my forehead just at the hairline above my eyes. It's an everlasting reminder of how awful war can be. It was a time of my life that I did not want to remember and tried to suppress it but my daughter Marilyn urged me to share it with you.

Our duties would change from time to time. We didn't know why, we just did what we were told. We soon found ourselves being shipped out to an Army Field Hospital. We were issued a duffel bag for our personal belongings which consisted of three pairs of underpants, three pairs of socks, two bras, Army fatigues, one pair of boots, a helmet, mess kit, toothbrush, and comb. That was pretty much it. In training camp Vera used to make jokes about it.

Typically, we wore one outfit and laundered the other. Laundry was not an easy task. In winter, when it was freezing outside, the clothes would never seem to dry. Other times there was no water for washing, so we would have to wear dirty clothes for a while.

The helmet, or bucket as we called it, was also our sink. We filled it with a cup of water, if we were lucky we might get a cup and a half, and if even luckier we might get hot water. With this water we would brush our teeth, then wash our bodies and faces, hair was last and we washed it if we could. Yes, believe it or not, we could wash our whole bodies with just a cup and half of water!

Our Army fatigues were pants and shirt; men and women wore the same. At 4'10" tall, my fatigues were always way too long. After a while I got frustrated with rolling up the pant legs and sleeves, so I started cutting them off. I had to use a belt to hold the pant up. We were definitely not making any fashion statements.

It seemed that every day was bad. I was in a unit close to the front lines. The sounds of the bombing were not only frightening but deafening. I hated the sound and prayed every day to have it end. We could hear the artillery or cannons whistling in the distant, the sound of the gun fire, and at times we could even hear the voices of soldiers in the distance.

We did our job. We couldn't run, there was no place to go. Besides, those wounded and dying soldiers needed us. That was our purpose. I just focused on helping the guy lying in front of me. Many were missing an arm or leg; others would not make it all. I knew that I may be the last person that they would see or hear. I did my best to smile, even though I was scared to death, I did it for the soldier. Many of those soldiers didn't ask to be there. They, like me, were taken from their loved ones and told to fight for the cause. It wasn't their cause; it was the cause of an insane leader.

One day we woke as usual to the sounds of the war. Got up and got busy with our duties. But, today was different, the artillery fire seemed closer than usual. We were ordered to evacuate our location; the Russian Army was advancing on us. We got busy. I was with one of the last groups to evacuate; there were about ten doctors, nurses, and drivers. The heavy artillery was landing closer as we rushed to load the wounded into the ambulances and grab whatever supplies we could get our hands on. The others had already left in ambulances loaded with wounded. The heavy artillery was now hitting the tents behind me as I helped load the last wounded soldier into our ambulance. One shell hit not far from us but we continued to work feverously to get out of there.

It seemed hot. My bucket felt heavy on my head. The bucket was always too big for me and would flop down into my eyes. Sometimes I would place a couple pair of underwear inside just to help hold it up. I reached up to wipe my forehead of what I thought was sweat. As I brought my hand down, I saw the blood. My Blood!! I don't remember anything after that.

Later I was told that the guy next to me, maybe a doctor or the driver, caught me as I passed out. I was put into the ambulance along with the wounded soldiers and we sped off just as more heavy artillery came in, destroying the entire Army Field Hospital unit. The doctor removed a piece of shrapnel from between my eyes at the hairline. He put a butterfly binding on it and wrapped my head in a big bandage. Then he put the smelling salts under my nose, woke me up, and told me to get back to work. He had lots to do and he needed my help. Hours later in another Army Field Hospital after we had taken care of our soldiers, the doctor called me over to examine my wound. He removed the wrap from my head, put in a few stitches, and said "You are one lucky lady." That's when I heard the whole story. He told me that the piece he removed was about one inch long and I was lucky that it didn't penetrate the skull. It was a fragment thrown out from a bomb shell that went under the lid of my bucket. The bucket slowed the shrapnel down and kept the injury from being far worse.

I'm sure there are other stories but please don't make me drag them up. Those fighter aircraft made a certain kind of sound. Even today I will hear a similar sounding airplane flying overhead, catch my breath, and it will send me back in time — especially the CalFire airplanes that fly low to fight the fires. I hate the sound of truck backfire and fireworks. I have learned to tolerate the sound of guns, but I still don't like the sound.

Wartime is Ugly

War was a tough time for my family. Each one of us had to choose a path to survival.

The last letter I received from my mother in 1945 is still with me today. I treasure that last communication, not knowing if I would ever see my mother or my family again. You can see a photo of the letter in Appendix 3.

The German Gestapo had taken my father, Karl, for being outspoken against their policies. As mother would say, "he just couldn't shut up." He always stood tall speaking his mind and was a little too outspoken against the Nazi regime, German policies, and the war efforts. This made him very unpopular with the authorities. Presumably, he was taken in for questioning but he never returned home. No one knew where they had taken him. It was relatively early in the war; mother didn't want me to worry, so she didn't tell me that papa had been taken.

This was about the same time that I was transferred into the field and assigned to my first unit at an Army Field Hospital. Hitler's Gestapo came to the village of Jaentsdorf shortly after, taking all the able-bodied men they could find. If a man resisted, he would be shot right there in front of his loved ones. Maybe it was for the best that papa was already a prisoner. The Gestapo took what they wanted, looting, pillaging and worse. This must have been a hideous and scary time for my family.

The Burgermeister had been drafted sometime earlier along with his two older sons. The Wallsteins were a well-respected family in our village. The Burgermeister is the senior political leader of our town, like a mayor. The Burgermeister's wife was still living in Jaentsdorf with her three younger children. The Nazi Gestapo shot her in front of everyone, including her three small children, for no other reason than she was the Burgermeister's wife. And, they could do it.

After that, my mother would hide in the hay loft or cellar on the farm when the Gestapo came into town. The fear of being discovered or trapped if they burned the buildings was forever on her mind. She had my five younger siblings with her the day she tried to flee. The Army stopped her and took the two horses, Hans and Gretchen. They left her with the old oxen and the cart. She was only a few miles from the village, so she turned around and went back to Jaentsdorf. Others in the village had already fled to other areas. The village was like a ghost town.

A few weeks later mother got word that the Russian Army was advancing their way. It was rumored that the Russian invaders would do even worse things than the Germans. It was hard to imagine how anything could be worse than what they had already gone through. But mother knew that for the sake of her children she should move forward as fast as she could to stay ahead of them. This time she left nearly everything behind, never to return to her beautiful home, shop or barn again. Once again, she loaded the cart with the old oxen to pull it. She packed what small provisions she had along with the two smallest children and headed west. Mother and the older children had to walk.

Unfortunately, politics and war left them with no path to safety. One evening they stopped to rest for the night. They found two little girls that had been left behind inside of a barn. The girls were incoherent from starvation and dehydration. One was nearly unconscious; the other was delirious. Their blankets were a mess. Their long hair was matted, filthy dirty, and covered in head lice. Mother cleaned them up the best she could as her own children stood in silence and watched. Mother asked Gerda, my older sister, to cut off the girl's long hair. Mother found some herbs growing around the old barn and brewed up a type of tea which she used to get rid of the girl's head lice. She fed all the children taking little for herself. During the night one of the little girls died. Mom buried her. The other little girl turned out to be the Burgermeister's daughter, Erica Wallstein. On the road, a few days later they met one of the Wallstein relatives who had come back to find Erica and they took her with them.

Mother was taking her children west toward the British and American lines with hopes of a better chance to survive. The oxen moved slowly and the cart didn't seem to make much progress. They were joined by other refugees. Then the German Army redirected them back to a refugee camp. My mother and all the younger children would wait out the war in that refugee camp.

It hadn't taken mother long to figure out she was going to have to protect her children from the cruelty of war. Gerda was too young to be drafted but old enough to be subject to the perils of wartime. She was a "budding teenager" and developing fast. Mom cut her hair short to look more like the boys which would also make it easier to keep a watchful eye out for head lice. She wrapped Greda's breasts and dressed her like a boy. Explaining to her that she must act like a boy or the soldiers would take her away and rape her. Fortunately, with Gerda's larger frame, she was able to pull this off. The ruse worked but it also meant that Gerda had to do manual labor and work in the fields with the other boys.

Arnold was the oldest boy, approaching thirteen. Mother depended on him to help her with the three youngest children. The Nazi soldiers wanted him working in the fields as well. Mother pleaded with them to let Arnold stay with her. She tried to explain that she needed his help with the smaller children, especially since the baby was so sick most of the time. There are times when it makes no sense why people do what they do. In war time it is even worse, and when some people get a little power they can become down right mean and cruel. That is what these soldiers were. They took Arnold out in front of Mother and all the other refugees, and broke both of his legs. The Nazi soldiers threw him on the ground in front of my mother and spat, "There. Now he can stay and help you." They laughed and strode off. An old doctor in the camp helped my mother to make splints and reset Arnold's legs as best as they could. Most days there was little food to eat and they were always cold, especially when winter came. Arnold's legs did heal but it was slow and they were never quite right. Arnold helped mother as much as he dared, without the possibility of getting the soldiers angry with him.

Renate came down with a horrible rash. There were no medicines or medical care in the refugee camp. Mother relied on her herbalist skills. If she were home in Jaentsdorf she knew she could have made a poultice of cornstarch to cure the rash. But there was no cornstarch to be found in the refugee camp and her little girl was crying from the pain

31

of the rash. Mother saw that potatoes were for dinner. She made a starch from the potatoes creating a poultice dressing to apply to the rash. Renate stopped crying, in a few days the rash began to disappear, and was soon gone.

As the war dragged on Erna, the baby of the family, became sicker. Erna had lots of problems. Her ailments could have been the usual course of nature or due to the ugliness of the war — malnutrition, unclean water, poor diet, and more. Nazi physicians were performing human experiments on prisoners in concentration camps and on the people in refugee camps. The Nazi physicians and their assistants would force medical tests on men, women, and children. History has shown that many of these tests were really medical torture, often resulting in death, trauma, disfigurement, or permanent disability. In the case of my baby sister, when the Nazi Physicians found out about her ailments, they sent soldiers to get her. They took Erna away from my mother. They were experimenting with transfusions and did a total body exchange of her blood. Considering the crude techniques, non-sterile environment, and unknown condition or compatibility of the other person's blood it's amazing that she survived. Erna was returned to my mother with only a brief explanation of what they had done. It was, as mother said, "By the will of God that my baby survived to grow up." Soon after, the war would come to an end.

As the war was winding down, the American and British soldiers moved into areas where the Nazi camps had been. The cruelty of what the Nazi Party did to their own people was evident. Cruelty to not only the Jews but to whoever ended up in their refugee camps and prisons.

The Red Cross set up shelters to help people. Soon they were trying to find and connect loved ones in every town or city. The Red Cross posted names in many different locations. All around there was nothing but destruction from the bombing and shooting. Beauty had been stolen from the towns and the land.

My mother, sisters, and brothers would once again find themselves on the move. They were directed to a resettlement camp in the area of Gera, Germany. Mother didn't know what to do. She was not allowed to go home to Jaentsdorf. Papa was missing. She didn't know where to turn.

The resettlement camp was not far from Wolfersdorf where my Uncle Mo and Aunt Ema lived. Aunt Ema was papa's sister, mother's sister-in-law. Every day Uncle Mo checked the posters that the Red Cross displayed in the villages; these signs listed the names of people displaced by the war. Uncle Mo saw the name of Selma Kranz with five children listed. They were reunited through the Red Cross and came to live with Uncle Mo and Aunt Ema in the small village of Wolfersdorf. Uncle Mo continued to check the signs every day. He never gave up hope.

Escaping Nazi Germany

It was cold that February of 1945. I had been serving as a transportation assistant for the head nurses of the German branch of the Red Cross for nearly three years. I hadn't seen my good friends from training camp, Vera and Sofie, in so long that I wondered if I ever would see them again. Drafted at sixteen, living with war and wounded at seventeen, I wondered what life would have been like without this ugly war. Now eighteen, I wondered, "Would I still be alive to celebrate my nineteenth birthday?"

Our train headed to Dresden. Dresden is situated in a valley on the River Elbe, near the Czech border. The main German Red Cross hospital was located there and this was where we brought the wounded out of the field from the front lines. My job had three main elements. First, just a short distance from the fighting, I would help at the Army Field Hospital loading wounded soldiers into an ambulance to take them to the nearest train. Second, we would remain with them on the train and see that they were transported all the way to the hospital in Dresden. Third, we were asked to assist at the hospital in Dresden if help was needed cleaning up the soldiers, administering medicine, and applying fresh bandages or clothes. If we were lucky we might get a small break and a chance to clean up. And if we were *really* lucky we would get a nice bed to sleep in for the night and maybe even see a movie. That didn't happen very often; mostly we headed back to the front lines the same day we came in.

Dresden was a beautiful city filled with a lot of art and fine culture. The city had been spared from air attacks and showed little sign of the war that was raging so close around it. It was steadfast in its beauty. If not for the lack of food and absence of the usual city hustle and bustle, I could imagine for a moment that this awful war didn't exist.

It was Tuesday, February 14, 1945, a day I shall never forget.

It seemed especially cold, that kind of wet cold that settles into your bones. I was on the train. It was a day like so many others, I had made this trip many times over the last few years, I knew it well. The bump and clatter of metal wheels on the tracks mingled with the deep low moan of wounded soldiers and refugees.

Today the fighting was extremely close to our train, I worried for our safety, then the moan of a young wounded soldier jarred me back to my reality, my job. I started getting the soldier ready to be unloaded for the short ride to the hospital. I couldn't help wonder what would become of this young soldier; how wrong this war was, how it had changed everything. I loved helping people, but I hated what the German leaders were doing to us. I no longer understood what the cause was even about.

We finished transporting the soldiers to the hospital. It was a lucky day; we had time to take a quick shower and get into clean clothes. It felt so good to be able to shower and wash my hair. Two other girls and I headed back to the train station. We had orders to return to the front lines the same day. We were nearly at the station when sirens started blaring in the distance, air raid sirens. We ran toward the train station as fast as our legs would carry us. The station was on the outskirts of Dresden, which may have been our saving grace. The heart of the city took a merciless beating from the bombers.

The British Royal Air Force and the U.S. Army Air Force were sending in waves of bombers filled with high explosives and incendiaries. There was no place to go for safety; the cellars were full. The sound of explosions was growing more deafening. The growl of large heavy bombers flying overhead mixed with the whistling sounds of bombs dropping, people screaming, and the smell of everything burning. The ground shook under our feet as we ran for cover. Soon the midday sky was no longer blue but a dirty black gray as smoke billowed into the air blocking the sun. Even the heat from fires cut through the February cold, which was unnerving.

We found our way to the station. We knew the route well. As we approached, we turned back to look at the heart of the city as the bombers were striking. We saw the bombs being released and exploding ... destroying everything in their path. Not knowing if the train station was a target, we made our way under a large train trestle bridge. A doctor, two girls, a couple of civilians, and I huddled together praying for safety as those bombs dropped nearby. It was so bad; my ears were numb from the noise. We spent six hours under that trestle bridge; it seemed like a lifetime. We were covered in black soot and I only knew that someone stood next to me when I could see the whites of their eyes. No one spoke. But my mind never stopped, always filling with thoughts. Lots and lots of thoughts raced my head. Past. Present. Future. Bombs. Family.

That train trestle may not have been the safest place; it provided good shelter but it may have also been a prospective target for the Allied Forces. It was a large bridge with six tracks going across it. God answered our prayers that day. We did not take a direct hit on that trestle.

As quickly as the bombing started, it all went quiet, a thick sort of eerie quiet. Our ears were numb from the bombing; we couldn't hear anything. There were no alarms going off. No fire wagons rushing into the streets. It was dark with fires burning everywhere. Toward the heart of the city there was a horrible red glow, as beautiful buildings were turned to ash and rubble. Our shock withdrew slowly as sounds of people moaning and crying "Oh my God!" filtered in. At times I heard something that sounded like thunder as buildings continued to collapse all around the area. We stayed put until morning.

With the first light of day, we could see the real devastation. Everywhere we looked, this beautiful city was now utterly destroyed. Sixteenth century churches at the heart of the cultural center were no longer standing. The Allied Forces aimed to break the morale and spirit of the German troops and German people. They did just that. Most of us were in shell shock. Our ears rang and pounded for days afterward. *When the terrorist attack of 9/11 happened in 2001, it brought back all these memories. Those dazed and shaken survivors from the World Trade Center attack looked just like us.*

Somehow, I found part of my troop: three girls, an ambulance driver, and the doctor that I had been with under the trestle. The others who had shared that space under the trestle bridge left to find their loved ones.

We stood there looking around and talking about what we should do. We realized this could be our opportunity to escape. Yes, maybe we would be captured. If captured by the Allies, we wouldn't have to fight anymore. If captured by the Germans, we would be sent to jail for desertion or killed. We were tired, dirty, and in shock. We didn't really know what to do; we had always followed orders. The old doctor became our commander. He would lead us to safety. So, we began a journey, heading toward Austria, and hopefully toward freedom.

I no longer remember the doctor's name and I feel bad about that. He was an older gentleman and feared for the safety of us girls. Under the circumstances he did an excellent job. He felt that we would have a better chance in the Austrian Alps. There would be more places to hide from the Russian and German troops. If we were lucky we might get caught by the Allies or maybe we would just wait out the war. A big fear was the Nazi SS. The biggest fear was the Russians; we heard all the horror stories of what the Russian troops did to the girls. It was unimaginable.

That first day we walked about twelve miles with no supplies. We traveled with other people initially but soon decided that wasn't safe for us or them. A larger group would draw attention and we were more than refugees, we were deserters. So, we split off on our own, following the rails or small roads that weaved between the small villages scattered along the way. The doctor seemed to know the way.

August was the name of the ambulance driver, we called him Gussy. He talked about his family and his dream of seeing them again. He was always so positive, giving us hope, and not allowing us to get down. We walked every day. We had no idea what might be waiting just around the corner. We relied on word of mouth for safe passage to avoid the Gestapo.

Don't ever generalize that all Germans were Nazis. We were deserters. If we were captured we would be taken to prison, tortured, or killed along with those who helped us. Germany and Germans DOES NOT equal NAZI. You can see what happens under a corrupt ruler. It can be very terrible.

Walking in the country along the back roads would lead us to many different places. I was the smallest at 4'10" tall and would often be sent to a house to seek food or a place to stay for the night. I guess they thought I looked like a child or less threatening. Most of the time the door was answered by an elderly man or woman. They would often ask me in but I would explain that I was traveling with friends and that we didn't want to be a burden. I would tell the story, providing only enough detail to determine if the family was friendly or not. Almost everyone tried to help, giving us a little something to eat, allowing us to spend the night in the hayloft, or directing us to a safer location. When we stayed the night, we would leave the next morning before the light of day as if no one had been there at all.

The doctor was not in good health and sadly he died on our journey. The poor man had trouble breathing; the long walks and cold weather were too much for him. We were in a small village when the doctor died, the villagers helped us bury him. I think of him every February.

After the doctor died, Gussy took the role as our commander and was instrumental in getting us to Austria. He taught us to distinguish between the different sounds of Allied planes versus German planes. We were good students and learned the various sounds of war. Gussy picked out places that were safe to travel and to stay at night. We learned quickly who was friendly and who was not. Sometimes one or two of us would approach someone in the town and talk with them briefly. They would either give us directions or say, "follow me". It worked on trust.

The people in those towns provided assistance but we were careful not to put them in jeopardy. They would spare some butter, honey, or bread. Some would even make us sandwiches; whatever they could spare. If they didn't have food for us, they might offer a sweater or a coat. Life was a hard struggle. Many folks had lost their gas stoves as metal was confiscated to help in the war efforts. If we learned that German SS (Schutzstaffel or Protection Squad) were in the area we would move on, wouldn't stay and wouldn't be seen. Families helped by supplying us with civilian street clothes and helped us move safely in or out of town. They always wished us good luck as we went on our way. Many of the families were in a similar situation with boys and girls from their town who were on the front lines or working behind the lines. They hoped that someone would do the same for their children.

When you give, it will be given back to you.

We safely traveled through the Alps, covering over 300 miles. It was the of heart winter. The air was frigid. But, we finally made our way to Graz, Austria. This was the town where Sofie lived. We were given shelter at a school. A very kind person told me that Sofie was working not far from where we were; she had written to me some months earlier saying she was back home. After I got freshened up, I walked to her office. Her boss greeted me and sent word for Sofie to come down. It was a very emotional reunion. Her boss excused her for the rest of the day.

Sofie took us to her mother's home. Her home was in a little valley that once had a paper factory. Sofie's father worked in that paper factory and had been working there the day it was bombed. She lost him. Her family home was too small for all of us and, besides, they were worried about German troops. Sofie's mother told her to take us up high into the Alps. We could safely stay in one of the mountain cabins that were used by herdsmen and their families during the summer months when they grazed their cattle and sheep in the high country. The cabins were locked up for the winter and no one goes there. The cabins had plenty of cheese and Sofie would bring us bread, butter, and root crops to help us get through the harsh winter. We hoped this would be a safe place for us to wait out the war.

It was getting more and more dangerous for Sofie to make the trip up the mountain to bring us food and news. She was worried about getting caught or leading Russian troops to our hiding place.

Surrender

We stayed in the mountain cabin high in the Alps near Graz, Austria for over a month. One morning Sofie came with the news that the Russians were advancing toward the town. We knew we had to do something. That afternoon we discussed our options: stay, move to a more remote location, seek asylum in another country, or find Allied troops. We heard that the Americans were near Vienna.

We all felt the need to move and agreed to head to Vienna. I pleaded with Sofie to join us, but she insisted on staying with her mother and said she would be okay. Early the next morning, before light had broken, we packed the cheese and bread we had, splitting it amongst us. We left that mountain cabin high in the Alps and headed northeast toward Vienna. We had been told that the American troops had set up a station there.

We carefully traveled through town, stopping only long enough to thank Sofie's mother and sister. From there we headed into the woods with the hope that we had not been seen by anyone. The rest in the mountains outside of Graz gave us new strength, hope, and resolve to reach freedom.

Many people were fleeing Germany, Russia, Poland, and other oppressed areas. Most people traveled alone, or in small trusted groups, like ours. Occasionally they would join a caravan with others, especially as they neared American or British lines hoping to reach freedom.

We had traveled by foot for three, maybe four weeks, changing course to the northwest to avoid German or Russian troops. We came across an old bus. It still had some gas but wasn't running. Gussy was good with mechanical things and messed around with it. He tinkered with this, jerry rigged that, and low-and-behold, he got it running! We all climbed in and Gussy said, "We won't stop until we find the Allies." We came across the Autobahn. Finding the bus and now the Autobahn was going to accelerate our journey ... one way or the other.

The autobahn was in pretty bad shape from all the fighting. We found we couldn't travel quite as fast as Gussy had hoped. The road was filled with deep pits and pot holes from all the fighting. Overpasses laid across several sections of road and we would have to find a way around them. We maneuvered around yet another pile of rubble when we came under siege from a small military unit.

Our hearts sank. We didn't know who they were. We hoped that because we were dressed in civilian clothes that we would be treated as refugees.

It was a small group of American paratroopers. It was a black unit. None of us had ever seen a black person before. At first, we were frightened because we could only see the whites of their eyes and teeth. Their commander realized what was happening and explained, "We are the night fighters and that was why we dress this way". The soldiers treated us with respect, telling us it was going to be okay, and that we were in safe hands. They took us to a refugee camp a few miles away. Once more, God answered my prayers.

It had been an arduous journey. My small trusted group had become like family. We had now traveled nearly four hundred miles together, mostly walking, and most of it through the Alps. A journey to freedom that took nearly three months from February to April of 1945. There were times of great uncertainty, exhaustion, and fear before reaching the safety of the Americans lines. Walking in the Alps was beautiful at times, like the escape of the Von Trapp family in the movie, "Sound of Music". But it was also very difficult. For me it was real.

Surrender was a great relief. I didn't know what would happen next, but I was sure it would be better than being caught by the Germans or the Russians. I worried about Sofie and her mother and sister.

Many of the American soldiers looked at us with great pity. But we were glad to be somewhere safe. Our prayers had been answered. We had done everything right, trusting God to get us to safety.

Once in the refugee camp, we were seen by a person who wrote down a lot of information about us — our name, parents, hometown, and lots of other things. I don't remember all the questions, I just answered them. Later I was worried that I might have said the wrong things. After all, I was now a P.O.W. (prisoner-of-war).

The food in the refugee camp was straightforward. There were a lot of refugees and they had to make what food they had stretch to feed everyone. I remember eating soup, lots of potato soup. When I arrived in the camp I was 4'10" tall and weighed eighty-five pounds. No clothes fit; they just hung on my small frame. The mess hall Sargent was a massive guy and a happy man. When he first saw me, he said, "You are nothing but skin and bones. You need to eat." He sat me down and gave me a huge meal. Eat I did. I ate and ate. I ate so much that I got sick, really sick. I had not eaten very much solid food during those long months walking in the Alps. My poor little stomach didn't know what to do with all this food. Now I was in sick bay. That poor Sargent felt so bad. It didn't take long before I was feeling better and was sent back to my tent.

The weather was starting to warm, it was getting near the end of May. We hadn't been in the P.O.W. camp at Siegendorf very long. I was sitting just outside my tent when

I heard my name announced over the loud speaker. My first reaction was, "It's over I'm going to be taken and executed for desertion or something worse. It's the end of me. I'll never see my family, let alone have one." They came for me in a Jeep and told me to get in. I was shaking. I could hardly move. I was so gripped with fear that the soldiers had to help me into the Jeep. I just knew it was the end of me. Fear raced through every inch of my mind and body.

The soldiers drove me to the building that we entered when we first got into camp. It was the Red Cross unit. The girl said that they were having trouble reading my tag. She made it clear that I couldn't go back home to Jaentsdorf. The area was now occupied by the Russians and as far as they knew my family had fled, hopefully ahead of the Russians. The girl explained that the Red Cross wanted to reunite with me my family, if they could. After a lot more question and answers, the soldier took me back to my tent. What started out as one of my worst days soon gave me new light and hope.

Others in my group were even luckier. All of them found their families and would be going home. My heart was filled with both joy and sadness as I bid my four companions goodbye. I felt all alone now and wondered where my mother, brothers, and sisters might be. Had they escaped Jaentsdorf before the Russians invaded? Had any of them survived? What about papa? Mother's last letter was my only connection to my family and became my closest treasure. I would read it again and again, praying and hoping that the next time they called my name it would be to join my family too.

As the days grew warmer and I spent more time talking with people at the camp, both refugees and staff. The Red Cross realized that this poor lonely soul (me) could be of great value to them. I knew just enough English to help with translation for the staff and, more importantly, the refugees trusted me. The camp was filled with people from all over

Germany, Russia, Czechoslovakia, Yugoslavia, and beyond. The Red Cross' objective was to "sort" people in the camp. Grouping people from the same country, province, or town provided comfort for the refugees in their shared language and heritage. It gave them something familiar to connect with so that they might locate friends and ultimately get reunited with their families.

The Red Cross was an important connection for me. I had worked with a German Red Cross unit before surrendering. Now I was working with the American Red Cross to help reunite families. I gladly and gratefully accepted the chance to help. This gave me a purpose for living.

Figure 4: My Red Cross Uniform, 1945

Ruhpolding

In the summer of 1945 I still had no word about my family. I would never give up hope. I heard from Sofie and, as she promised, she was doing ok. The Russians had entered Graz but were there a very short time before the British military arrived. It must have been a horrible time for her but she wouldn't speak about it. Sofie had also heard from Vera. I was so happy to now be getting some mail and to be reconnected with my friends.

I had been steadily working with the Red Cross for several months. I was also taking English lessons each evening from one of the Red Cross staff, working to improve my understanding of the language. Word came that I was going to be transferred to Ruhpolding. "What next?" I thought.

Ruhpolding was where the American soldiers would come for R&R (rest-and-relaxation). The hotel had been taken over, functioning as the R&R center for soldiers needing rest and waiting for new orders.

In Ruhpolding I became an official member of the Red Cross. I was not considered a P.O.W. any longer. Ruhpolding had a working hospital, staffed with real doctors and nurses. I was given a real uniform and a place to stay. I had a real bed, a roof over my head, and three square meals a day to eat.

My job was to collect information on each G.I. as they came in for examinations. I was still learning English but was improving quickly. I thought it was funny that they called the soldiers G.I.'s, a sort of nickname meaning government-issue. I was busy. There was a lot of paper work. I seldom looked up at who came in or went out. I had to concentrate on what I was doing because English was still not that easy.

We didn't go out much. There was an 8:00pm curfew. As part of the Red Cross there were stringent rules to follow or you would be out in a heartbeat. One of those rules was 'no fraternizing with the troops'. I took all this very seriously because my new position meant a lot to me. Even though I was no longer considered a P.O.W., I was still a refugee in search of my family. I was all alone. I didn't know what my future would hold. But as Grandma Emilia had taught me, "Believe in God. He has plans for you. Trust in Him."

I quickly grew to love Ruhpolding. It is nestled in the Bavarian Alps. For me, it was a magical place. A vast meadow was dotted with tiny houses and American tents. A stream ran down along the back of town. An artesian spring bubbled in the center of town with icy cold water that tasted like heaven. A beautiful little chapel still stood on a hill beside the small village. It was the most beautiful place in all the world.

Summer quickly past into fall and then into winter. When the snow began to fall, it became even more beautiful. I took advantage of a pair of skis left on the little balcony of my room. I would ski whenever I had a chance, often joining others on outings in this frozen wonderland. We also ice skated on the little creek when it froze over.

It had now been seven months since my little trusted group had surrendered to the American paratroopers and were taken in at the refugee camp. The rest of my group were home somewhere celebrating with their loved ones. As for me? I felt blessed. I had a place to stay and a good job. I longed for my family but I was happy to be alive and in such a beautiful place.

The snow was beginning to fall outside the mess hall when we arrived for our evening meal. There was a little extra excitement in the air as it was Christmas Eve. We just sat down at the table to eat when we heard the crackle of an announcement coming from the loudspeaker of a Jeep outside.

The mess hall quickly got quiet. A number of people stood up to listen. It seemed that we were all holding our breath in unison. No one knew what it might be.

Over that loudspeaker, for the troops and the entire village to hear, came the announcement, "The curfew has been lifted. The church will be open tonight for midnight services." Like so many, the little church in Ruhpolding had been nailed shut by the Nazis who had occupied the area earlier. The Americans removed those boards and nails, opening up the church with help from clergyman in the area. As the announcement finished, the church bells began to ring for everyone to hear. It was the most beautiful sound you ever heard, especially after being silenced for so many years. This was the Americans' gift to the people that Christmas.

I'm not sure if I ever finished eating. I was excited. There were tears of joys and hugs from everyone. The store keeper opened up his shop and gave out all the candles he had, so that we could carry them to the church that night.

It was gently cold that evening. Great big fluffy snowflakes were falling, the kind that catch on your eyelashes as they float and flutter to the ground. At 11:00pm, I walked with others from my Red Cross command, holding that little candle. I don't really know how many people were there but it seemed like hundreds of us. We sang Christmas hymns as we walked up the hill to the church.

The church was tiny with a steeple that soared into the heavens. It was the kind of church that welcomes you when you first see it and hugs you as you walk through the door. It was incredibly joyous and tearful. When we arrived, the church was already packed tight inside with people standing outside. No one minded; the joy was profound. People came from every corner of the region — town people, soldiers, nurses, doctors, country folk, everyone. It didn't matter, young and old, the candle light just kept coming.

The glorious sound of church bells ringing blended with the joyful voices of all the people. It stopped snowing for a while and the stars joined the celebration, shining brightly. It was the greatest gift. I looked up, thanked God for that night, and prayed that my family was safely together someplace.

After the service we walked back to the village singing and laughing with so much joy. The merchants in Ruhpolding opened their doors to everyone, adding a gift of their own to the evening. We enjoyed hot chocolate, coffee, or tea along with pastries. It was like a dream. It was later than most of us had stayed up in years; it was 2:30am and we didn't want it to end. It still fills my heart with joy when I think of it.

Christmas Eve in 1945 will be etched forever in my mind. It was a fairytale dream come true.

Meeting Marvin

We were blessed to hear the bells of the church ringing every Sunday now and life felt more positive. Curfew had been raised to 10:00pm. By this time the British and French Troops had already pulled out. The British pulled out first, followed by the French. The Americans troops were also beginning to pull out, many getting ready to return home. The Americans combined zones and the Army Core of Engineers were there to help start the rebuilding process; rebuilding infrastructure, railroads, bridges, and more.

It was the beginning of January 1946 and I was on desk duty as usual. I was pretty comfortable with my job now, taking information from the dog tags — names and numbers. I registered each soldier, filled out the paperwork, and filed it once their examination or physical was complete. Some soldiers would be called back, if follow-up was required. It was a hectic time as new troops were always coming in. I really couldn't tell you when I first saw Master Sargent Marvin Phillip Bodle, but it was probably in the midst of one of these busy times.

Marvin was from Wyoming, wherever that was. Bodle is a Scandinavian name. When Marvin first came to Europe, he was part of the Third Wave at Normandy. The Army Core of Engineers were responsible for the construction of roads and bridges to get equipment across rivers as fast as possible. Marvin had been in Germany for nearly three years.

When he was stationed in Rheingau, Germany, helping install a bridge for the Allied troops to cross the Rhine River, his outfit came under attack. After being treated at the Army hospital Marvin came down with a nasty chest cold, so they sent him and a few others to Ruhpolding for R&R. He came in multiple times to be seen by the doctor. The doctor told one of the nurses, "That guy has a different kind of sickness." After Marvin was given a clean bill of health, he still came back. I mentioned to one of the nurses that this soldier's name kept showing up, the nurse said, "Yes! He is a special kind of sick boy." Well, I still didn't get it.

Figure 5: Master Sargent Marvin Bodle, 1946

One evening, one of the American nurses suggested that we go over to the new recreation center. When we arrived, the girls walked over to a table that seemed to have just enough seats for us next to some soldiers. The American nurses slipped into two empty seats leaving one left open for me. Marvin stood up and pulled the chair out, offering me a place to sit. After being introduced, he ordered me a Coke. We sat and talked, maybe even danced, but I don't really remember. Later I realized it was all a setup between Marvin and the nurse.

Before I knew it, it was 10:00pm and curfew time. The MPs (military police) came around to escort us girls back to our quarters. Marvin walked outside with us and once we were in the Jeep, he jumped in too. When they dropped me off, he said, "I'll see you." He would say this every time we parted after that.

There was a strict curfew at the center. There were lots of rules, but none were too hard to follow. If it was after dark, an M.P. would take us home. Refugees and the troops were not supposed to fraternize, but it happened anyway.

Marvin always seemed to show up wherever I was. I was smitten but also terrified that I would lose my position with the Red Cross. He assured me it was okay, but I was still terribly nervous about it.

Marvin had trouble pronouncing my first name, Herta. Soon he began calling me by my middle name, Hanna. As long as he called me, I would have gone by any name! The name Hanna seemed to fit everyone else's liking as well and from that time forward I have gone by my middle name, Hanna.

We had known each other for only three months. Every chance Marvin had, he would ask to take me out, even just for a short walk. Sometimes he sent word by messenger that his driver would pick me up at a certain time to take me someplace. His driver's name was Johan, and the Americans called him Joe.

On my twentieth birthday, March 29th,1946, Marvin had Joe, his driver, pick me up and take me to Deggendorf. We spent a beautiful afternoon walking and talking. Marvin told me he was being transferred to Regensburg, on the confluence of the Regen and Danube Rivers. I was deflated, thinking, "Well that's the end of that." I liked being with Marvin and now he was leaving. I felt a sense of loss.

Figure 6: My Twentieth Birthday, March 29, 1946

That evening he asked me to marry him. He proposed at the mess hall in Deggendorf. As thrilled as I was, I couldn't say yes. We had only known each other for three months. He was the father of two children back home. He was a divorcee, something that was uncommon and frowned upon at the time. And even more … I still had no word of my family. I couldn't say yes: I couldn't leave Germany. I just didn't know which way to turn. I needed more time to think about it.

I talked with the girls back at Ruhpolding; they all tried to give me motherly advice. I wrote to Sofie and Vera, hoping their letters would help me make the right decision. I just didn't know what to do.

Thankfully Marvin was a very persistent fellow. "No" was not an answer he was willing to take. I finally agreed to marry him.

Our Wedding

In the few short months that led up to our wedding day, life took another twist. Shortly after accepting Marvin's proposal, I was transferred twice. I was released from the Red Cross post in Ruhpolding. Happily, I found another post near Regensburg, where Marvin was stationed. I went to work with a Red Cross Unit that was working with the U.S. Army Air Force. This assignment turned out to be very short because an opening became available in Deggendorf which was only 46 miles from Regensburg, where Marvin was stationed. In the meantime, Marvin was transferred, sent by the Army Core of Engineers to build the main hospital in Ramstein, now separating us by almost 100 miles!

It was in Deggendorf that the head nurse and some of the others girls got excited about the wedding. I told them my story and they took me under their wings. The head nurse had some beautiful material from Italy. I don't know where it came from ... might have been from the black market. She had planned to take the material home with her but decided it was much better suited for a wedding dress — my wedding dress! She was so ecstatic when she presented it to me. I was thrilled; it was beautiful. Marvin's driver Joe knew a seamstress in town who said she would be happy to make the dress. With a bit of bartering, Joe also found the veil. He traded some coffee, sugar, and chocolates for it. Somewhere a pair of high heels became part of the ensemble. Joe was amazing.

I clearly remember meeting with the Military Chaplain. He sat us down and had a very long talk with us, both individually and together, before he would agree to marry us. This was the first American-German wedding he would be performing; he wanted to make sure we fully understood what we were getting ourselves into. He was soft spoken, yet very assertive. "You need to think about the differences — the different life styles and religion, the difference in where you each came from, and your different cultures. You need to think about what each of you have been through and how it could affect your relationship and judgments of each other. How will the boys react to having a new mother? Hanna, what will you think or want to do when you receive word of your family? Marvin, how will you handle people's reactions to your new German wife? How will you both respond to the American people that may not fully understand who you are?" There was so much more said. There was so much to think about. It was a big decision and a big commitment.

When the Chaplain was finally done with our interviews and was satisfied that we both understood what lay before us, he agreed to marry us. His final words were, "Your love for one another is strong. As long as you both stay focused on that love, believe in God, and stay strong in that faith; you can make it work. But you <u>both</u> must always work together to keep it that way. No one person makes the marriage alone. You are entering into a partnership for life and must always work on it together."

With everything in place, the date grew closer. I grew a bit more nervous too. There still was no word about my family and it was now a little over a year since my surrender. The Red Cross posters looking to reunite families were still being updated and displayed in public places. My name was on those posters. I prayed with the Chaplain at our first private meeting. He gave me words of encouragement to not give up hope. He said that he would keep me in his prayers. Each time I saw a new list, I would stand before it, reading, and hoping to see the names of my family.

On Saturday, August 24th, 1946, we both dressed simply. I wore a simple little suit that I had. Marvin wore his uniform. We drove to the Burgermeister's office in Erlangen. It was a very simple ceremony with just Joe, Marvin's driver, and one other person as witnesses. This German civil ceremony was necessary because I was still a German citizen. Tomorrow would be the big day.

That afternoon we rehearsed for the church wedding to take place the next day. Then we retired for the night.

Joe was a wonder! I don't know how he managed to find all the things he did. He liked Marvin. He also would translate for Marvin. If Marvin needed anything, he would somehow find someone to do it. Joe even made arrangements for wedding pictures to be taken. It was a bright sunny cold day. I remember being cold. The photographer pulled out a fur wrap and placed it on my shoulders just before snapping the photo.

For our wedding, Joe, or Johan in German, presented us with two beautiful hand-painted wooden plates that he had made. This amazing man was a driver, artist, and magician at finding things. Marvin gave Joe two silver dollars; he took those silver dollars somewhere and came back with matching wedding rings. *Unfortunately, many years later we lost those precious wedding rings in Wyoming. Marvin lost his ring while gutting an elk and I lost mine doing diapers, both very honorable work but not particularly pleasant.*

Figure 7: Joe's Wedding Gift, a Hand Painted Wooden Plate, 1946

Our wedding was more of a dream. It came together because of the friends we made and the people we worked with at the time. I honestly believe that if it had been left up to us to figure it out, we would have just slipped off quietly and gotten married. This was the first American-German wedding in the area and it meant a lot to many others besides us. The girls I worked with at the medical core and the engineers that Marvin worked with had big plans to make this a special day. And a big day it was! Marvin seemed to know everything that was going on. As for me, I just sort of went with the flow. It was as if it all took place in a dream. I can't even recall the fittings with the seamstress for the dress.

On Sunday, August 25th, 1946, we each arrived at the little church near the University of Erlangen. It was a simple church that had managed to withstand the ravages of war. The windows still had their beautiful stained glass, handcrafted centuries before. Even the pipe organ still worked. It had not been hit but was not in very good shape. The girls from my medical corps found some fresh flowers and ribbon, decorating the church, making it look beautiful.

Marvin wore his dress uniform. He was even more dashing than I remembered. I was amazed that this man wanted to marry me, when I was sure that he could have had any other lady out there.

Figure 8: Our Wedding Day, August 25, 1946

Joe brought me to the chapel. He handed me a beautiful bouquet with two long white gladiolas and two smaller ones. He told me that the gladiolas represented our family, the long ones for Marvin and me, and the two smaller ones for the boys. He said, "This is my way of bringing your family together." He had been praying for us. He prayed that he would also find his own family, separated by war, and be going home. He was always so positive and upbeat. He reminded me of Gussy, the ambulance driver, who had brought me safely to this point in my life making all this possible.

I stood at the door of that little church with the chief head surgeon of my unit. I asked him if he would give me away. The bride's maids were all girls from my unit. It seemed like a fairytale. The dress had been custom-made for me by a seamstress in the town, she was part of the wedding along with her three beautiful children. The veil was a long trailing one and the little girls helped carry it. I barely remember what took place, it was all a delightful swirl. Later, I was told that many of the townspeople came out as well. They stood just outside the church, perhaps wanting to see something happy and beautiful for a change.

When the wedding was over and all the pictures were taken, we hopped into the waiting Army Jeep with Joe at the wheel. Following us to the reception was a long wedding procession made up of many more Army Jeeps. The reception was in the small village of Pottenstein just below the castle of Gossweinstein. It was about an hour's drive along steep, narrow roads. The Army Corp of Engineers had located their new R&R center there for officers' rest between assignments. It was referred to as "the country club". The Behringersmuhle Lodge, where the reception took place, was a lodge owned by an elderly couple, at least we thought they were elderly. They had an eight-year-old daughter who also helped serve at the reception. *We stopped in to see the Lodge on a visit in the late 1980s. It hadn't changed much. When we met the young forty-five-*

year-old woman who ran the resort we found out that she was the owners daughter and remembered the wedding.

When we arrived, the Behringersmuhle was set for the grandest of parties, the officers made sure of this. The head chef worked wonders, baking a huge wedding cake. There was so much food. Several of the GI's brought out their instruments and played music for us to dance, sing, and enjoy. At some point alcohol began to appear. Some of the people in the party got pretty drunk, including our driver, Joe. I don't know the details but somehow, he managed to wreck the Jeep. We partied late into the evening.

We stayed at the Behringersmuhle Lodge for a few delightful days together. There was a little stream that twisted and turned through the area, filled with beautiful German brown trout. Marvin would go fishing. I would foolishly catch grasshoppers for his bait. Every morning I would end up wet from my toes to nearly my waist from wading through the tall grass covered in morning dew. I did it several mornings so it had to have been fun ... or love. Marvin always brought the catch back to the lodge and the chef gladly cooked them for us. We also drove up to the castle at the top of the hill. An old church stood across from it; Marvin marveled at the beautiful architecture and paintings that adorned the ceilings and walls. The church was quite large, so it had a real honest-to-goodness pipe organ in it. When it was played, the sound carried out over the valley below for all to hear. The sound was fantastic. *Many years later it was very special for Marvin to share the sights and sounds of this old church with our daughter Marilyn during our 1983 trip.*

A few weeks after the wedding reception we went to Pottenstein, it was a get-away or a kind of second honeymoon. After that we returned to Erlangen which would be our base and new home. We lived in base housing for the officers. Housing came with a maid. It was the first time and probably the only time in my life that I had a maid. A servant was something that I just could not get used to.

First, it was only the two of us, Marvin and me. I could do everything myself, so it just felt foolish. The girl worked with several families in the base housing unit. We soon became very friendly and she was helpful too. She helped me learn my way around and we would go shopping together. I was grateful for her help and friendship.

About two weeks after the wedding Joe got the news he was praying for and dreamed of hearing — they had found his family. He was in seventh heaven. They were all safe and were now living in another town. He immediately asked for leave and headed off to be with them, leaving Joe behind to return as Johan to his family. The day he left was sad; it felt like a large part of our life was going away with him. I had only known the man for eight months but he had done so much for Marvin and me. We had become a family of sorts. Now Joe was leaving. We were happy that he was rejoining his family but also very sad to see him go. Wherever he went I know he must have done well with his positive upbeat attitude and thrifty ways.

From Europe to the U.S.

We settled into married life living on-base near Erlangen. We started making plans for our future and that of our sons. Marvin wanted to continue his work with the Army Corp of Engineers so he decided to sign up for another term of three years. We began making arrangements to bring his boys, Bill and Phil, to Germany to live with us.

Marvin traveled to Nuremberg periodically to attend some of the war crime trials. He didn't say much about what was going on at the time, only that "it was a big thing". I wrote to Sofie and Vera regularly. They were dear friends and were helping me search for my family. I also continued to work at the clinic in Deggendorf. Life was good.

The process for getting Marvin's two boys to Germany was not very clear. Marvin was working with the school principal in Sheridan, Wyoming, where the boys went to school. The principal acted as a counselor for families of soldiers overseas. We also worked with the Red Cross in both Germany and America to help bring the boys here with us. The boys were living with Marvin's parents after the divorce. Marvin had been sending money home to his mother to help her care for the two boys. He made sure that she always had enough to clothe and feed them, with a little extra to cover medical expenses or other things she may need.

As Marvin's part in the war trials at Nuremberg was winding down, we got word from the school principal that there was "trouble brewing" with his two boys. He wrote that Marvin's ex-wife was giving his mother a lot of trouble over the boys. Marvin concluded that she must have caught wind that there was money involved.

Marvin's ex-wife left him while he was overseas in service. He was so grateful that his mother stepped in to take care of the boys, since his ex- had all but abandoned them. The principal said that his ex- was stirring up a lot of trouble for Marvin's mother and may even try to take some legal action. All this mess was also blocking the way for the boys to come to Germany.

I remember how torn he was. Marvin was flustered and frustrated, at times openly angry about it. He spent lots of time talking with legal counsel about all of it before he finally told me everything that was going on. His ex- had managed to block the boys from coming to Germany and was trying to get custody of them. Legal counsel advised him that if he remained in Germany, she would have a good chance of winning.

Marvin feared for his sons' lives. He said his ex-wife was "a very irresponsible woman". He had already lost one son, his youngest, to "her wild and reckless ways". He said, "I will not lose the others."

It was with a heavy heart that Marvin requested to be dismissed from his duties and asked to return to the U.S. as soon as possible. At first, I was taken back by all of this. But, now I was getting a clearer picture of why he was divorced. It also made some things that the Chaplain said in our pre-nuptial counseling clearer — things about "starting the paperwork" and that "there was much to do in a short time" and "you both must always work together."

I was also not quite feeling myself. After a medical checkup I learned that I was pregnant with a child due in May. We were both excited over the news of the baby. Yet the joy was troubled with this black cloud hanging over our heads. Everyone assured me that it would all be okay, it wasn't the end, but a new beginning.

Before I knew it, Marvin was shipped off with another group to the U.S., and he would be home in three weeks. My paperwork was not yet complete. It would be a month or more before I would be able to start that journey.

Authorization for relocation was slow. There were many people returning to the U.S. along with new people going to the states, like me. Husbands always went ahead of their brides, returning home with their troops or other forces. The wives would wait until there was space available on a returning ship. This was 1946 and the passenger airplanes we have today just didn't exist. Passage between Europe and the U.S. was done by ship. The ships were the same ones used to transport supplies back and forth; they were not luxury cruise liners but quite crude and primitive by anyone's standards.

Thankfully, I was mostly past morning sickness and could finish my immunization shots. I completed my health checks and the mountain of paper work. I packed what few things Marvin and I had, crated, and labeled them to be shipped. Standing there looking at the crates, I began to weep. Our once happy little home was just a crate going to an unknown place. I wept. I sat and cried for a long time. I wrote letters to both Vera and Sofie giving them Marvin's mother's address and telling them that I would be leaving for Bremerhaven the next day. I explained that I wasn't sure just when I would get to that northernmost German port, but that I would send word when I did and let them know that my precious little one and I had made it safely. I cried myself to sleep. I was not only missing Marvin's strength but I missed my family so much.

In the morning soldiers came and took the crates away. I had time to say goodbye to the maid and my neighbors. A short time later a driver arrived to take me to the train station. He gave me instructions and my papers, saying, "Goodbye and good luck, ma'am. Have a safe trip home." Home? Yes, I guess I was going "home".

I found my train, climbed aboard, and took a seat. Riding the train north into the next step in my life. In my heart I acknowledged that my whole family had been wiped out by the war, that I was the only one left. This was God's intention for me. It was not a bad plan. I was going "home". I was soon to be a mother of three, counting the little one I was expecting. I was going to America, a place my father had so fondly talked to me about when I was a small girl. I would always hold on to those precious memories of my family. Whenever I felt sorry for myself, I would remind myself that I didn't have to suffer as they must have. My parents would want me to be strong, that was how they had raised me, and not to feel sorry for myself, like I was doing now. I wiped the tears away and said, "You can do this. Do this for all of them."

When the train rolled into Bremerhaven, I left the relative quiet of my car and was immediately confronted with the hustle and bustle of a seaside city alive with activity. A woman in uniform met me and a few others. She took us to where we would stay for the next two weeks, waiting our turn to depart. There was still more paperwork to fill out. There was another round of shots; more health checks. I was amazed at the number of new brides waiting to go to America. Each morning I would wake to the sounds of the sea gulls squawking, fog horns blaring, and the smell of salty sea air. Each day we met for a briefing; if our names were not on that day's list we would be released to spend the day as we wished. I often walked around the harbor watching the ships and the sea life at this busy port. I would find a bite to eat and sometimes take in a movie. There were a few shops, but I didn't have much money to buy extra things and besides there wasn't anything I needed.

It was early October when my name finally came up on that list. I was given a final briefing along with my boarding pass. It was getting cold; the days were growing shorter and gray along the sea. We stood in line a long time waiting to board that small supply ship heading to America. It was a long line of women, each with a small suitcase and hand bag. We were placed six to a room, or maybe eight, with a bathroom down the hall, not far away. We were taken in small groups to our quarters and assigned a bed. Luckily, I was placed on a bottom bunk. A Chinese girl was assigned the bunk above me. After we settled into our quarters we were allowed to go topside to watch as the ship readied to leave port.

By late afternoon the ship pushed off from the docks, moving slowly, heading toward the English Channel. I was swept with a feeling of remorse as we left Bremerhaven and Germany behind. I sensed that I would never see this land again and that this chapter in my life had now ended. What was before me? I didn't know. I could only pray that it would be good.

The ship moved slowly. On either side of us were two smaller ships looking for underwater mines left behind in the war. These minesweepers would escort us all the way out to the open sea.

Once our ship moved further from land into deeper water, the weather got cold and it looked like a storm was brewing. The ship was starting to rock as the waves grew larger. Everyone was ordered below deck. After dinner that first night I went right to bed.

The next morning, everyone in my bunk room was feeling sea sick. The Chinese girl in the bunk above had very long hair. In the night her hair would come loose and she was too sick to keep it tied up. Her hair kept flopping down and swishing across my face, adding to my nausea. Out in the open ocean, the ship went through a series of storms that seemed endless. We were in rough seas without any break. During that period, I just couldn't take that long hair anymore. One night, I grabbed her hair and tied it to the bed frame. Well, that poor girl had to throw up and tried to get down off her bunk but got all caught up with her hair being tied to the bed. She threw up all over the floor. I was desperately trying to untie her hair which she was pulling on and screaming at me in Chinese. She was slipping on the floor and couldn't get loose. Her screams brought a lot of attention to our cabin and people came in to see what was happening and to help. By the time they got her all untangled and taken out of the room ... well, let's just say it wasn't charming. I got reprimanded for tying her hair to the bed. I do think all those guys were laughing about it after it was over. We all forgot about being sick for a while too.

It took thirteen days to cross the Atlantic Ocean and reach America. I was sick the entire time. Our cabin stunk and no one cared. We just wanted to get off that rocking and rolling pile of metal. We didn't eat or even drink much water during that voyage, nothing would stay down. It left a lasting impression on me ... I HATE BOATS AND WATER TO THIS DAY.

When the ship entered New York Harbor we were not standing on deck to see it. I don't remember what time of day it was or anything about it. I spent two more days in sickbay in New York City. I was severely dehydrated and they were concerned about the baby. They put me on intravenous rehydration to get me back up and going; I think it took several days. My baby and I were fighters. The Red Cross sent a message to Marvin letting him know that I safely arrived in New York and was being treated for dehydration. Once I was able to walk without feeling like I was going to fall over or pass out, I was released to my quarters to prepare for debriefing, immigration, and introduction to New York City.

New York City was (and is) an overwhelming place. I spent two weeks in New York City and saw lots of places thanks to the Red Cross. The Red Cross organized sightseeing trips for the new brides arriving in New York. I saw Grand Central Station, had lunch at the prestigious Waldorf Astoria Hotel, and drove through the amazing tunnels, both the Holland Tunnel and Lincoln Tunnel. I wasn't able to climb up in the Statue of Liberty but I did get to the top of the Empire State Building. The fog was so thick when I went to the top of the Empire State Building that I couldn't see a thing. Honestly, that was probably good because I don't particularly like heights.

I saw Ellis Island from a distance. I wasn't processed through Ellis Island because the Red Cross brought all the immigration paperwork to me while I was in sickbay.

Ellis Island had been closed during World War II as very few immigrants were being allowed into the country and resources were all redirected to the war effort. Ellis Island had fallen into neglect and abandonment years earlier, after the Great Depression. By the 1930s, more immigrants were leaving the U.S. than arriving. When I came into New York, Ellis Island was used for other purposes, enemy merchant seamen were detained there and it was a U.S. Coast Guard training facility. Later, Ellis Island reopened for immigration in 1950, then was officially closed in in 1954. *In the mid-1980's work was done to construct a memorial wall at Ellis Island and a request was sent out for people to commemorate family members who had been processed there. For Christmas 1987, all my beautiful children had my name engraved on the 'Wall of Honor' at Ellis Island.*

It was November and New York City was getting pretty cold. I had been well taken care of by the Red Cross and had everything I needed, including a warm coat and pair of shoes. They took us to so many places and showed us things that I would never see again. But, I was there and can say that I have been in Times Square, went to the zoo, and walked in central park.

How can I ever say "Thank you" to the Red Cross? They had been a huge part of my life for four years. I will always be beholden to them. Here I am in America. Now it's time for the final part of my journey from Europe to the U.S. to start my new life with Marvin.

Wyoming

One morning in mid-November one of the Red Cross escorts came to me with a small package. It was my tickets to Wyoming. This would start the final leg of my long journey. The Red Cross had been schooling us on the customs of this great country. They were helping us understand what to expect as well as how to react so that we would fit in and feel comfortable in our new home, this great nation of ours.

I had received a few new clothes. My body was changing as the baby was beginning to show. I was taken to the train station and they explained what to look for. I would be making the rest of this trip on my own. They gave me some money and a small package with food and drinks. I bid goodbye to my new friends, thanking them for everything they had done. I took a deep breath, boarded the train, and found a seat.

The seats on the train were hard wooden benches, not the soft cushiony ones that we have today. I would be sitting on these hard-wooden benches for miles and miles, day after day. The train filled up with lots of people, some were refugees, others just Americans heading to Chicago or wherever. As the train rumbled along we talked amongst ourselves and it was quite nice. I met people like me from other parts of the world, refugees hoping to start a brand-new life here in America. We all had big dreams.

When the train left Illinois heading toward Nebraska, there were not as many people on board. More people got off than got on. The next leg of the trip was a long one and took a couple of days. We made a few stops along the way; people would get on and off at each stop. Everyone was polite. I would spend most of the time during the day watching the ever-changing country side. At night I would try to sleep as best as I could. The train moved through hills, around bends, along rivers, and around lakes. There were endless stretches of farm land and beautiful small towns. Now and then the train would stop long enough to be able to get out, get some fresh air, and stretch my legs.

I was glad to get to Omaha. We had a longer lay over and spent the night. I was happy for a warm meal, a bath, and a good night sleep on a bed, not a hard-wooden bench. In the morning I felt ready to start again. The next stop would be close to home, Clearmont, Wyoming, wherever that was.

I settled down in my seat for the final leg of the journey. Just before the train started to roll a man made a grand entry into my train car. He was tall, wearing a cowboy hat, and had a saddle on his shoulders. The spurs strapped to his boots jingled as he strode into the car. He flung the saddle up into the luggage rack above me, tipped his hat, and said in a deep voice, "Howdy, ma'am." He sat down on that old wooden bench, stretched his legs out, pulled his hat over his eyes, and was soon snoring away. At first the smell of sweat from the saddle was a bit strong but I got used to it. That cowboy didn't wake up until the train pulled into Gillette, Wyoming. When the train rolled to a stop, he once more tipped his hat, grabbed the saddle, swung it up on his shoulder, and said "Goodbye, ma'am." It was my first encounter with a real honest-to-goodness cowboy.

As the train rumbled through Wyoming, I knew this was my new home. I was looking out the window as we rode through miles and miles of prairie; flat, empty, and desolate prairie. What happened to all that green and beautiful county? I thought, "This couldn't possibly be where I was heading." There were a few wild animals and cows scattered about, but there were no trees and nothing was green. What would happen next, I wondered as I rubbed my stomach and my baby?

It began growing dark which was almost a welcoming rest from the bleak landscape. The rocking of the train lulled me to sleep and I dozed off after the cowboy left. The conductor came around, tapped me on the shoulder, and announced softly, "This will be your stop, ma'am." It was quite dark outside now. I was nervous about what would come next. I was excited to see Marvin. I was looking forward to meeting my new family. I kept telling myself everything would be okay. As the train came to a stop at the tiny little Clearmont station, I stood up, took my bag down from the luggage rack, pulled my coat tight around me, and started for the door. I was the only one getting off the train at Clearmont. The conductor helped me down out of the car. On the landing stood a small woman with two little boys, one on each side, just under a gas lamp.

Josephine, Marvin's mother, had walked to the train station with the two boys. Marvin had to work that night and could not get away to meet me. He sent his mother and the boys to meet me and get me home safely. It was a bit awkward at first. There we stood; four strangers about to start a life together as one big family. Josephine broke the ice, came forward and introduced herself, then introduced Bill and Phil who were a bit shy and standoffish. It was dark and cold and I hadn't had much to eat all day. The boys carried my bag, handing it off between them as we walked into the darkness. It was a short distance to their home, and the old house was warm and welcoming. Once inside Josephine took my coat, sat me down at the table, and gave me a bowl of stew, talking all the while.

She explained that Marvin would not be home until very early in the morning; he was working a swing shift job and was very sorry that he couldn't be there to meet me. I really don't recall if Hugh was there or not, but I'm sure he was. After about an hour Josephine put the boys to bed. She showed me to my sleeping quarters, saying "Now you get some sleep. Marvin will be here early in the morning and I'm sure that you two have a lot of catching up to do. Goodnight." Then she was gone. I stood there all alone in that little space for a bit. I cleaned up, crawled between the covers, and was soon sound asleep.

Somewhere in the early morning hours Marvin came in and crawled into bed. I remember cuddling and gently crying as we held onto each other for what seemed like hours.

The next morning, I saw what was hidden in darkness the night before. Nothing. There was even more nothing. The landscape was barren in the Powder River area where they lived. Nothing significant grew, only a few straggly cottonwoods trying to survive. Hugh and Josephine's house was a three-room log cabin with two bare light bulbs hanging from the ceiling. They were blessed with cold running water inside, but the bathroom was out back. The train station was within a stone's throw as Marvin would say. We lived there for about three weeks until Marvin found us a house in town that was available. Hugh and Josephine had four children; Nina, Hugh Junior, and Marvin were still living, but Corey died in childbirth.

Clearmont was a typical cowboy town. It wasn't much. No fancy houses. The only telephones were at the school, the general store, and the mayor's office. Mail was delivered twice a week; we picked it up at the post office which was located in the general store. There was an old gas station where Marvin worked after high school, before going into the service. It seemed that nearly everyone could fix a broken-down car in this country. If they couldn't, they would hitch the car to a horse, pull it into town, and leave it at the gas station to get it fixed, or so the story goes. *Today, the main road by-passes the tiny town of Clearmont.*

Figure 9: Hugh and Josephine Bodle Family, 1946

Josephine, Junior, Nina, me, Marvin, and Hugh (seated)

It took time for the local folk to warm up to me. Some would just stare at me like I was from another planet. Some made little remarks about Nazis, because they thought all Germans were Nazis. But they did begin to warm up to me after seeing me with Marvin and the boys. They were happy to see Marvin smiling and laughing again. The older generation, those who fought in World War I, were among the first to welcome me. Others who were immigrants or had grown up with Marvin also accepted me, especially the other men who had gone off to fight during that time.

Marvin's brother, Hugh Junior, fought in the South Pacific. Junior, as everyone called him, had been in Japan before returning home. He was drafted right out of high school at eighteen, arriving back home just a few weeks ahead of Marvin. Most of the folks in town reached out to help Junior resettle back into civilian life.

About three weeks after I arrived in Clearmont we moved into our own place. Marvin found a little fixer-upper to purchase. It had two bedrooms and came with a wood cook stove. Unlike Josephine and Hugh's house, we had no indoor plumbing so we had to go outside for the outhouse and to fetch the water from the pump; no complaints from me. These were minor inconveniences. We were happy to be able to do what we wanted and not be under someone else's roof. Marvin quickly decided that the winter weather was way too cold for us to go outside for water so he installed running cold water into our little house.

We were a family of four now, almost a family of five with one on the way. Bill was four years old. **William Hugh Bodle was born August 11th 1942** to Marvin and Deloris. Phil was three years old. **Philip Landon Bodle was born September 14th 1943** to Marvin and Deloris.

Bill and Phil began to learn that if I said something, they had to listen. As for me, I had to learn to be firmer with them and not so soft or they would quickly walk all over me. It was not an easy adjustment for all three of us, but we made it work.

Bill was a good-looking lad with big blue eyes, fair skin, and blond hair, a lot like his dad's. He loved being outside, fishing and playing in the water. Bill loved to read and could often be found with a book in-hand and another on the ground next to him. He was smart and witty, with a smile that could melt your socks off. Bill tried hard to make me feel welcome and often helped me out, bringing me things he thought I was looking for or helping me find words to express my thoughts. Helping Bill and Phil with their school

74

work really helped my own English to improve. My reading skills improved along with theirs. It was wonderful, yet challenging, for all of us. Bill loved animals and we always had plenty around for him to care for and to love. He was a big help on the farm and with the other kids.

Phil was a handsome freckle-faced kid with big blue eyes and blond hair. He was full of life and into everything. He loved to be outdoors and his favorite past-time was fishing. He would rather fish than do anything else, especially if the 'anything else' had to do with work. Phil had a soft side and was a very generous soul. I had more problems with Phil than Bill. He was a strong-willed young man, much like his father. With their similar strong-minded natures, Phil and Marvin often butted heads.

Thanksgiving was something new to me. In Germany we celebrated the harvest in October. I learned that here we would celebrate with a big dinner and everyone would get together. I had never cooked a turkey like this before. I was constantly asking others how to cook certain things because there were so many dishes that I had not cooked before and some that were completely new to me. This year was extra special because we were all together for the first time. Marvin and Junior were home safe from the war. Phil and Bill had parents again. I was a new member of the family and expecting. It was truly special for me; it was an incredible feeling to once more be part of a big family.

Life took on new meaning and I began to settle into it. That first winter the weather was harsh and cold; the wind blew the snow deep against the houses. Yet when the sun came out, the snow would sparkle like a million diamonds had been scattered on it. Christmas was similar to those at home in Jaentsdorf. Josephine read the bible to us, we had a big feast, and would sing songs.

Marvin was still trying to figure out what he wanted to do. He didn't really like living in town. We celebrated Christmas in that little house in town but by spring he wanted out. Marvin heard that one of the ranchers wanted to move closer to town. Marvin met with him; his name was Glen Campbell, no relation to the famous singer. Marvin returned home, all grins, "Guess what, honey?" I looked up at him from whatever I was doing, not sure what I was going to hear next. He said, "I've made a trade. I traded the house for a ranch just outside of town, about four or five miles. Its two thousand acres. It's all ours. You're going to love it." He looked at me waiting to see what my reaction was going to be. I must have had a dumb blank look on my face.

Rancher Campbell wanted to retire and his poor wife was suffering badly with arthritis. They had two sons who had returned from the war but neither of them wanted to work the ranch, choosing to live someplace else. The Campbell boys weren't home for very long before they left, moving in different directions. Marvin, Junior, and I drove out to the ranch to look at this 'dream home'. As Marvin and Junior stood there talking excitedly about all their plans, I could see that the corrals were in far better shape than the old house. Marvin was very pleased with the exchange and kept saying "it's a beginning" and "everything will be perfect, just have a little faith." So, we swapped homes. Neither of us had much to move; we didn't have a whole lot back in those days.

Marvin bought the rancher's livestock. It was early spring on the ranch. I must say that cowboys are a strange sort. They live for the spring. It was calving time and roundup, which means branding time. These were all new things to me. I never did get used to the smell of burning hair and hide, the crying of the poor calf as it was struck with that hot branding iron. Nowadays they don't brand calves and just put ear tags on them. The bunk house had been taken over by chickens, so sleeping arrangements were somewhat odd that year.

A letter arrived from Vera. She saw the name of Selma Kranz on a Red Cross poster and tracked down her location.

This was beyond belief. I was stunned. I had given up all hope of finding my family alive. Was it really them? It had been so very long without any word. I read those lines over and over again. "There was a Kranz family that matched your family description in the small village of Wolfersdorf, Germany", Vera wrote. "I believe it is them. It looks like everyone has made it and you should try to write them and see." That first letter was difficult for me to write. What do I write to a family that I wasn't sure was even mine? Harder yet, was waiting for an answer. I prayed it would be them. I knew it would take at least two months for a return letter to make it back to me. Mail was still carried by ship across the ocean; airmail didn't exist yet, so I knew I would have to wait two months or more between letters.

I was getting huge with the baby. Getting around was getting more difficult and the baby kicked a lot. As my due date got closer, I worked to arrange everything. The hospital was two hours away and likely impossible to get there on time. Instead, I arranged for a midwife to take care of me, which was common in those days. The midwife's name was Maddie, short for Madeline. She had some problems with her legs that made getting around difficult for her, but she was a real sweetheart and knew just what to do. Maddie came out checking on me often.

I received a letter from Germany. It wasn't from Vera or Sofie. It was from my mother. I sat and cried for joy then anguish at how I had given up. Her letter told me just enough to confirm that they were all together and healthy. They decided to settle in Wolfersdorf and start all over again. Everyone was alive and doing well, under the circumstances. She wished me happiness and was so grateful that I had found someone who loved and cared for me even though it was so very far away. Just knowing that they were alive and well made the long wait between letters seem shorter. We wrote regularly.

On the last day of April, I went into labor. It's impossible to conceive what labor pain is like unless you have been through it. Thank God for Maddie. I had a long labor but finally with one last hard push, on Maddie's orders, I gave birth to the cutest little baby girl. Marvin was there with us when she came into this world. I remember counting her toes and fingers; don't ask me why, it was just something you did. She was pink and healthy in every way. Including her lungs, when she let out a bellow. This little baby and I started a journey in my homeland of Germany, nine months earlier. We rode the rough seas of the Atlantic Ocean together, saw New York, and traveled by train to be here with our family. There to greet her into the new world were two excited brothers, her grandparents, and her Uncle Junior. I told Marvin that if we had a girl I wanted to name her after my mother and my two best friends, and so we did.

On May 1st, 1947 Selma Vera Sophie Bodle was born on the ranch; it was our first child together.

Our sweet little girl had a very long name to honor my mother, Selma, and my two dearest friends, Vera and Sofie. We were now a family of five this beautiful blond-haired blue-eyed girl and two handsome blond-haired blue-eyed boys. I was so proud!

Life on the Ranch

Ranchers are a special breed and are always helping each other out.   Ranchers ride in to assist another rancher. Payback is that you ride out to help them too. They get together in groups for the roundups, helping each other cover the vast acres of land herding cattle and branding calves. Working together they can move quickly through one herd, then on to another ranch to do the same.

Milk for the Baby

During our first roundup in 1947, Marvin and Junior, along with the other men, were working the cattle on our ranch. They expected to be away for two or three days. I was still very new at being a rancher's wife, as well as being a mother. Our cow had stopped producing milk and Selma's feeding time was fast approaching. Like any new parent, I was fretting over what to do. Selma was still sleeping and the boys were playing close by, so I thought I could ride quickly into town, get some milk, and be back before she awakened.

I dashed out to the corral to get a horse. I remembered how to harness Hans from so many years ago in Jaentsdorf. This shouldn't be too difficult. I got the bridle down and walked over to the horse, whispering all the time. I told the horse what we needed to do and how important it was for us to get milk for Selma. The horse lowered its head and I was able to put the bridle on, followed by the saddle. I put a sack on the back for the milk and told the boys to stay put, keep an eye on the baby, but don't wake her or she will start to cry. I explained that I was going to get some milk and I would bring them back a sweet treat. I climbed up on the saddle and we headed to town. There were two gates between our ranch and town, so I had to get on and off the horse to open and close those gates on the way. Both times the horse stood patiently waiting for me.

When I arrived at the store I bought the canned milk along with a treat for the boys. Lloyd Snyder, who owned the store, helped me mount back up. He looked over the horse and handed me the sack. He asked how the horse rode. I said, "Fine. I ride him often." I rode back home, reversing the process and taking care of the gates along the way. When we got home, I first checked the baby and she was still sleeping peacefully. I gave the boys their treat and then took care of the horse.

At the end of the round up, Marvin stopped in at the store on the way back to the ranch. Lloyd told him about me riding into town to buy milk and about the horse. When Marvin got home he stormed into the house demanding, "What were you thinking?" I told him, in a matter of fact way, that the baby needed milk, he wasn't home, and not expected for a couple of days, so "What was I supposed to do?" His answer was "Ride the horse that's broken, not the green horse!"

It turned out that I had taken the wrong horse. There were two horses that looked alike to me. The one I picked was not fully trained. Marvin could never get on that horse without it bucking, yet I could walk right up to it. Lloyd said it was balance and a soft touch. I believe that the Good Lord was with me that day and the horse knew it could trust me.

Our son Bill wanted to go with his dad on a roundup. He talked nonstop about it and Marvin finally agreed that he could join the next one. Bill was six. This was a big step for him. He could hardly wait for the next day to arrive. He got up early, along with Marvin and Junior. He sat up straight and proud in that saddle with his little hat on his head looking like a miniature cowboy. I handed them their sack lunches, Marvin stuffed it into the saddle bags along with some water and coffee. They rode out to the next ranch, returning home the following evening. That little cowboy was exhausted and his legs were sore for days. But kids bounce back quickly and Bill was ready to go again.

The ranches of Wyoming are vast swatches of land. Many of them are thousands of acres, two or three times the size of ours. It could take days to ride the fence lines. There were miles of nothing before you would come to a ranch house, corral, and barracks set in the middle of nowhere. It was the same for us, except we were closer to town.

Just Over the Hill

The Rasmussen Ranch was our nearest neighbor. Shirley told me all about her place and that the ranch had been passed down through several generations in her family. I had not seen it but from her descriptions I imagined it as being beautiful. Our ranches joined each other. Shirley said it was just over that hill and that someday I should come over for coffee and visit. Shirley was engaged to marry Kenneth Bates. Marvin and Kenneth would ride the fence lines for one another or run into each other while riding the lines.

It was early June and the weather was good, not too hot yet. Marvin and Junior were out working the cattle in another section and I had finished up my chores early that morning. I looked around considering what to do next when I got the idea that this would be a perfect day for that visit with Shirley. After all, she had invited me several times. It would be polite to accept her offer. It can't be that far. Shirley always said, "It's just over the hill." We lived in wide open spaces. There were very few cars. This was a time before everyone had telephones. We didn't even have electricity on any of the ranches yet. So, I wasn't driving and there was no way to call Shirley to tell her I was coming over.

It was such a beautiful day and a nice walk would do us all good. I bundled up my baby girl, placed her in the buggy, took the Bill and Phil by hand, and we headed up the hill.

That hill was a bit steeper than I expected. When we were standing in the dirt road looking up toward the top I guessed it to be maybe a half mile to the top, at the most. The further we got up that hill, the steeper it got, and it turned out to be a mile, or maybe more. I kept reassuring the boys that once we got to the top we would be at Shirley's house where a cold drink and some homemade cookies would be waiting. Those two little guys helped me push that buggy up the hill with thoughts of some reward. I kept telling myself it would be worth it to have a nice visit and talk with another woman. I missed my girlfriends, the laughter, and those fun times.

The sun was now high in the sky as we reached the crest of the hill. The boys ran on ahead as I finished pushing the buggy up to the top. Then we stopped and just stood there, not moving. What a sight we must have been. The three of us just standing there, looking. Looking way, way down into the valley "just the other side of the hill." We could see Shirley's house and the other buildings. There were some trees around the house. The ranch was huge. The valley stretched off into the distance for as far as the eye could see and Shirley's house was right in the middle. It looked like a tiny little matchbox. I have no idea how far away it was. But, it was a very long way.

The two boys looked up at me with big eyes, as if to say, "We're not going to walk all the way down there, are we?" I looked at them, then back toward the valley and the ranch house. I turned, glancing back at our house which was considerably closer. Looking back at the boys, I said, "This isn't quite what I had pictured. Let's go home and bake some cookies. What do you think?"

Yes, you guessed it! We took hold of the buggy handle and made our way back down that hill to our driveway. The boys ran off to play while I made lunch along with fresh homemade cookies. Back home, in Germany, villages were very close to one another. Distances were nothing like Wyoming's wide-open spaces. It was a lesson I would never forget.

Later that day we told Marvin of our adventures and he got quite a laugh over it. That weekend we drove over to visit Shirley and Kenneth. They thought it was a funny story too. I'm glad that I can at least make people laugh.

Later that same summer Kenneth and Shirley got married on the ranch. It was my first American wedding. It was a real cowboy style wedding. They got married on the backs of their favorite horses. I would never forget it. I was Shirley's matron of honor and Marvin was Kenneth's best man.

The Prairie Fire

The summers went by quickly on the ranch. There was always something to be done — fences needed mending, a horse to be broken, gardens needed tending, always something. I was beginning to settle into this strange new way of life.

September arrived in a hurry. Bill was going into second grade, Phil was starting school that year, and this would leave me a little more time with Selma. School started on September 2nd 1947, the day after Labor Day. Clearmont didn't celebrate Labor Day; it was just another work day for us.

A week later, on September 8th a fire was started by one of the trains. No one was quite sure if it was caused by sparks on the tracks or cinders from the coal fire that powered the massive engine. The wind picked up and was blowing hard. I could see smoke and fire as it rolled over the hills in the distance. It was as if it was alive. New fires started ahead of the main fire by grasshoppers that would leap ahead of the flames just as they burst into flames themselves.

I was terrified. This monster was rolling straight for our house. I could see and smell the smoke; even feel the heat of it. The wind began blowing harder. Distant haystacks went up like torches. My mind raced, "What to do?" Marvin and Junior probably could not get back to us in time. If we went into the cellar, we might burn up or be trapped inside — we couldn't stay in the house. Then I thought of the shale shelf, just a short distance uphill from the house. It had nothing growing on it. Maybe we would be safe there. I quickly handed the boys towels, telling them to dunk the towels in the water trough. I grabbed Selma and her bottle, and met the boys by the water trough. The wet towels went over the kid's heads, on the only horse in the corral, over Selma's buggy, and one for me. We raced for the shale shelf.

The fire now reached the buildings. I could hear the horrifying yelps, screeches and screams of our farm animals, chickens and pigs that could not outrun the fire. An oil drum exploded. The sound of breaking glass as the house went up in flames. We didn't have time to look back. All we could do was run as fast as we could, trying to stay ahead of the fire. I swear it was licking at our backs. We felt its heat gaining on us. We reached the rocks, but now what? We couldn't see anything and we were enveloped in smoke. We huddled together and prayed out loud the whole time for God to save us.

Somewhere I thought I heard a motor and then a horn. Just when it seemed that the world was disappearing into a wall of thick black smoke, this car came flying through the flames, its driver laying on the horn. It skidded to a stop just inches from Selma's buggy. I grabbed the baby and pushed the boys into the car, barely making it in myself. We sped off, back through the wall of flames.

When we finally rolled to a stop, the back seat was smoking and everything around was black and burnt. Somehow, by the grace of God, one of the neighbors saw us running toward that rocky hill and came to rescue us. It seemed that everyone in our small community was waiting for that car to get back and when it did, they were all screaming and cheering.

Marvin and Junior had been out on the ranch trying to save the cattle by cutting the fence so they could run. When they got back into town later that day we hugged and stayed close together. Somehow, we all made it.

We went back to the ranch to look. Where our house and corrals once stood, now was only a pile of smoldering ashes. We found very few items, almost nothing was left. One of the two hand-painted wooden plates given to us on our wedding day by Marvin's driver, Joe, had survived the fire. The other one was destroyed. *I still have that surviving plate and treasure it (see page 57).*

We had to finish killing some of the chickens and a pig that were badly burnt but had not died. The horse was found and treated for minor injuries. On the hill, on the shale shelf, stood the remains of a burned baby buggy.

It was a massive prairie fire, burning over 40 square miles before it was over.

The people in our little town came together and helped us get back on our feet. They threw a benefit party and raised $67.70 (about $760.00 in 2018 dollars). That may not seem like a lot of money but it was HUGE, considering how little all of us had. The benefit was held just four days after the fire. It helped us get going; we had to start over. Thankfully, we were all still alive and together.

Big Goose Creek

The prairie fire was a mile marker. We often talked about things as "before the fire" and "after the fire". We lived temporarily in the barracks of an old abandoned prison camp in Clearmont. It was small and cramped but we were together and safe. Josephine, Marvin's mom, came back to live with us for a while. Josephine and Hugh had moved to Montana, near their daughter Nina, shortly after Selma was born.

Marvin never gave up. He was my rock to lean on and support me. Every day he would tell me, "Something special will come out of all of this, just wait and see." He kept looking and asking around if anyone knew of a place that he could move his family to. He worked every kind of job, no matter what it was, to keep us fed and to save for the future.

About three months after the fire, just before the holidays, it happened ... a ranch came available. It was a beautiful ranch built by an old German fellow. We rented the house along with some pasture land near Big Goose Creek, at the foot of the Big Horn Mountains. Local legend said that this area was a hide out for the James Gang, when things got "too hot" for them. Some even say that Butch Cassidy roamed this area too. For me, I thought I had died and gone to heaven. It was a picturesque and peaceful spot.

I never dreamed I would have such a beautiful place to call home. After the fire, I just felt like my life was not ever going to see happiness again. Now here we were in a house that seemed huge, especially after the little barracks of the prison camp. It had a huge kitchen with a built-in cabinet that you could access from both sides of the wall and a pass through. A creek ran through the property. It had a beautiful view and trees, yet it was close to town. Oh, how I loved it there. I still dream of it from time to time. If I had one last wish, it would be to go back and see this place. I was so happy at last.

I was now in the first trimester of pregnancy when we were able to buy a few head of cattle and started ranching again. It was at this time that Marvin's dad, Hugh, came back to live with us too.

The boys were in school. When the weather was good, Bill and Phil would walk to school rather than catch the bus. The road had an underpass for the creek and cattle. The boys spent a lot of time down there with their grandparents. Grandma Josephine loved to fish. She would time it just right to be down at the creek fishing when the boys came home from school. Marvin gave the kids a little school work incentive and promised them new fishing poles if they kept their grades up. It worked well with Bill, but not with Phil. Marvin kept his word, Bill got a brand-new pole along with a new tackle box for his efforts in school. All of us went down to the creek for his first lesson with the new pole.

I was getting bigger with the baby and busy with Selma who discovered that her legs and feet could take her wherever she wanted to go. It was warm and the fishing was slow. Bill soon became tired of waiting for the fish to bite and laid his new pole down on the bank. He went off to do whatever caught his attention, probably something Phil was doing. What happened next is a bit of a blur. Josephine started yelling. Bill and Junior lit into a dead run, diving toward the water just in time to grab the pole as it hit the edge of the creek. Grabbing it set the hook and Bill reeled in a beautiful German brown trout. Bill was hooked for life on fishing after that, so was his brother Phil.

In spring life came to the ranch, I saw so many things that I hadn't seen before, herds of deer or antelope mixing in the fields with our cattle and horses. It was amazing. Flowers were everywhere and I loved it. I had a small garden and planted flowers at the house. Big Goose Creek also came to life with lots of beautiful little springs and the sound of frogs.

Marvin told me to keep an eye on the kids because of the snapping turtles. I had never heard of a snapping turtle but the creek would soon be full of these strange creatures.

One spring afternoon, the boys were on their way home from school and spotted a giant lazy turtle sunning itself on the bank of the creek. As boys are, they were curious about it and went to investigate. It was a large turtle and didn't seem to want to move, so they began to tease it.

Marvin and Junior were by the barn shoeing horses when they spotted the boys. They saw what was going on but the boys were too far away to hear them. They knew they had to intervene before someone got hurt. Junior grabbed a shovel that was leaning against the barn. Marvin reached the boys first, yelling for them to stop and move away. He knew he had to put a stop to it, right then and there, because it was a very large snapping turtle. Marvin started explaining to the boys what could happen when Junior walked over with the shovel. Boom. In the blink of an eye that snapper had the shovel in its jaws and would not let go. Those two boys' eyes were as big as saucers by the time I got there with Selma in my arms. It took all Marvin and Junior's strength to drag that turtle to the water before it finally let go of the shovel and swam off into the creek. That shovel wasn't worth a damn for digging after that. The boys never did tease another turtle, that I know of, after that.

Edwin Marvin "Bud" Bodle was born on August 1st, 1948 on the ranch at Big Goose Creek. It was a joyous time for me. I wrote and told my mother all about it.

Edwin was born on the first day of August. He was perfect. Marvin wanted to name our first son together after his best friend growing up, if I didn't mind. I was okay with it, as long as his middle name was Marvin. Edwin Marvin was a chubby baby with big brown eyes and dark hair. It was the first of our children to look like me. It didn't take his Uncle Junior long to bond with him. Junior visited him every day. I would hear him say, "How's my little buddy doing today?" as he reached into the crib to pick him up. Before very long Junior had everyone calling him Buddy or Bud, the name stuck. Bud and Junior were inseparable, once he started walking Bud following Junior around in his little cowboy hat and boots; it was so cute.

Big Goose Creek was my happy place. Everything seemed to be perfect. We started talking about trying to buy the ranch. *I often wished we had bought that ranch but realize now that it would have changed everything that followed. My children wouldn't have met their mates and then I would not have all the beautiful grandchildren, great-grandchildren and great-great-grandchildren that I love so much.*

When we looked into buying that ranch we found that it was part of a large estate that was in probate. It was tied up in messy court proceedings between the heirs and the law. We had been in the Big Goose area for a couple of years, but it was time to move on. Our life had other adventures in store for us.

Homesteading Wyoming

Marvin and Junior received news of the Homesteading Act being applied to another area of Wyoming and open to the GIs. It was a lottery. Both brothers put their name into the lottery.

Junior received notification that he was one of the one hundred and fifty GIs, whose name was drawn in the 1950 lottery. He was number 97. Junior would receive two hundred acres of bare ground. I was relieved that Marvin had not gotten picked because I liked the Big Goose area. I didn't want to move. Marvin and Junior had other plans.

Marvin and Junior pooled their resources and before I knew it, we were moving to the Cody, Wyoming area. Marvin was very excited with the potential. We sold pretty much everything we had. Marvin and I raised the $1000 required for start-up (equivalent to $11,000 in 2018 dollars). Marvin and Junior were a team but with us putting in all of the start-up money they agreed that the deed would later transfer to us. The seed money we raised would give us the ability to drill a well, set up a shelter, support ourselves for a year, buy seed, and start our garden. If we were lucky we might even have a little money to buy some farm equipment. We were starting over again. We would build a home from scratch with lots of hard physical work, sweat, and tears.

The Bureau of Reclamation opened land for homesteading by veterans at Heart Mountain and at Riverton Midvale Irrigation District. We were drawn number 97 for homesteading land located on the Japanese American Heart Mountain Relocation Center, just east of Cody. It became available because the government no longer needed the land after the relocation center was closed in 1946.

Figure 1: Japanese Relocation Center, Cody, WY, circa 1944

Japanese American Relocation Center is a polite way of referring to the Japanese internment camps used in World War II. After Japan's attack and bombing of Pearl Harbor, President Franklin D. Roosevelt ordered the forced relocation and incarceration of more than 110,000 people with Japanese ancestry. More than half of the internees were U.S. citizens (62%) and people with as little as 1/16 Japanese heritage were placed in the internment camps.

The Heart Mountain Relocation Center had operated from June, 1942, to November, 1945, housing over 10,000 Japanese-Americans at its peak. You can find more on this unfortunate chapter in history at www.heartmountain.org.

We were chosen for a section on the lower bench, called Eagles Nest. There would be thirteen homesteads on this bench. Cody was to the west about sixteen miles away and Powell was about fourteen miles east. We went to Cody for nearly everything because it was a bigger, better developed town, as it was the county seat. Powell had the closest hospital, schools for the kids, and became the center of most of our social community life.

The day we arrived at the homestead site, Marvin was beaming with excitement, "This is home, honey." I looked up at my beloved husband in disbelief. All I could see was barren hills dotted with sagebrush and cactus. There was not one tree, nor building, to be seen for miles. I wondered what we had gotten into. Compared to Big Goose Creek, this was like landing on the moon. I was devastated.

In the four years that I had been in America we had been through a lot of life style changes. I thought I could deal with almost anything, but this was more than I expected. Where are we going to sleep? Where do we go to the bathroom? Where will we get drinking water? What am I expected to do with the babies ... surely there are snakes out here?

Marvin was my rock. He had all the answers, even if they were not exactly the ones I wanted to hear. Marvin and Junior soon had a spot cleared for the tent that would serve as home temporarily. He also set up a small enclosure so I could go to the bathroom with dignity.

We met others who were in the same boat. It didn't take long for the men to start working as a team. Our place would have the first well and became a gathering place for water until the others were able to sink their wells.

Figure 21: Delivery of the Old Barracks Building, 1950

Figure 32: Placement of the Barracks Building

We were each given an old barracks building from the internment camp. We worked together to put in a foundation for that old building. Winter was coming so everyone worked extra hard to get shelter for their families. The barracks weren't much, most didn't even have floors. It was basically a wooden box of four walls and a roof covered with black tar paper. The building we received would have housed more than one Japanese family. There were no interior walls to separate the families, and one wood stove for heat and cooking. At least it had a floor. It was hard to imagine how those poor Japanese people lived in them during the war.

Figure 43: Marvin, me, and all our earthly possessions, 1950

When the wind swept down from the Rockies across the open prairie, it found its way through every crack in those wood walls. That first winter we found out just how bad the Japanese families had it. We had been having trouble keeping the tar paper in place. One night the wind howled strong and the snow was coming down nonstop. The boys were bedded down close to the fire. Selma was sleeping in a large crate. Bud was in bed with Marvin and me. The weather was dreadful; we were in the middle of a blizzard. Sometime during the night Marvin got up to check the fire. There was a layer of snow all over the inside of the barracks. The boys were okay but Selma was buried completely under a thick blanket of snow. Marvin pulled her out, brushed the snow off, and put her in bed with us. The poor little thing was blue. We both rubbed her little arms and legs until she got her feeling back and was pink again. As soon as conditions allowed, we fixed the siding on that old building to keep the snow out.

Two years after taking the homestead, in the spring of 1952, that old barracks was beginning to look like a home. We joined with the neighbors to bring power into the area. Marvin put in a nice kitchen with a wood and coal burning stove for cooking and keeping us warm in the winter. We had a fancy outhouse; it was a "two-holer". The kids would say, "A big hole for big butts and a little hole closer to the ground for little butts and short legs." Marvin thought of everything! *We used that two-holer until Marvin built an indoor bathroom in 1957.*

We built a small house for Josephine and Hugh across from ours. Junior lived with them. There were no interior walls; Josephine hung sheets up as room dividers. Late in the spring of 1952 Josephine's sister came to visit. This was when we found out that Josephine was having health issues. I was now pregnant with my third baby. Thanks to her sister we learned that Josephine was bleeding. We took her to the hospital in Powell, much against her wishes. Shortly thereafter Marvin and Junior drove her to Billings, Montana where she passed away from Ovarian Cancer on the 2nd of June.

Marilyn Carmon Bodle was born on the 9th of June, 1952, our first baby born on the homestead. Marvin surprised me with a crib he had made for the new baby. We were now a family of seven.

She was a cute little blond, blued-eyed baby. It didn't take her long to have daddy wrapped around her little finger! Marvin named her after his favorite movie actress at the time, Marilyn Monroe. I gave her the middle name of Carmon after my dear friend and neighbor, Carmen Hirst. Carmen had done so much for me during my pregnancy and through the very difficult time of losing Josephine, Marvin's mother.

Marvin and Junior went into town to pick up supplies. There was a store in Powell called Gambles Department Store; it had everything you could think of or want. I am not sure what they really went into town for, but when that old pickup came rolling into the driveway it was loaded down with a whole new kitchen set up. It had a brand new electric stove, oven, and refrigerator. Marvin and Junior were grinning ear to ear. This would be the year of my first modern appliances. We were all excited.

As time went on farm buildings began to multiply. Corrals were built. Fences and cross fences were put up. I planted over two hundred trees and shrubs that we hoped would grow to create wind breaks. We planted a small garden. We were required to make improvements every year to continue to qualify for the Homestead Act. We divided the land for specific purposes. Later, on the spot, where Josephine and Hugh's house stood, became the central garden area that provided most of our food.

Marvin and Junior farmed the land and raised livestock. We grew mostly beans, alfalfa hay, and grain. We would alternate some of the fields with corn or potatoes. Neighbors helped each other at harvest times because we didn't have any specialized equipment, especially for harvesting corn and potatoes.

Marvin was always improving the old barracks and turned it into a beautiful house. He added a big utility room and bedrooms on the back, expanding the house to four bedrooms. He enlarged the living room on the side and added a mud room as you entered the house. Phil built a beautiful wall unit of shelves and cabinets for our new living room when he was in high school.

We became very close to all our neighbors. We were always helping each other out. My closest friends were Carmen Hirst and Lee Powers. We would get together to celebrate everything from birthdays to weddings, baby showers and the harvest. Celebrations usually included music and dancing. I love to dance, especially polka and waltz but square dancing was foreign to me. Marvin knew all the dances. He was a great teacher and made it fun for me. I did finally learn to square dance and looked forward to it. I would practice with Carmen, Lee, and the kids.

Allen Lee Bodle was born on July 28th, 1953. Carmen and Lee gave me a fantastic baby shower.

Allen had blue eyes and blond hair. He was a lively little guy and was always on the go. His middle named came from one of our neighbors and good friend, Lee Powers. Selma liked to carry Allen around. He was crawling and walking before he was a year old. Allen was forever getting into things … and out of things. It was hard to keep him in the stroller; he would climb out, disappear, and get into things he shouldn't. Marvin made a little "leash" to keep him from running off when we went shopping; it was a belt with a loop on the back that we could tie to a rope. Some people thought we were being mean, others thought it was pretty clever. For us it was necessary, to keep him from getting too far away.

Entertainment was sitting around the radio listening to music and stories. It was a new tube radio and the latest technology. We didn't have a television. Story hour on the radio was a favorite. We would gather around the radio and listen to stories like the Green Hornet, Superman, or Dick Tracy. That was great entertainment.

My sewing skills improved; I would make or remake everything. I often sat up late at night, after the kids were in bed, sewing little girl dresses and boys' shirts or pants. We did a lot with a little. I took old clothes apart that other people didn't need and turned them into clothes for our family. Together with friends and neighbors I learned to quilt. One of the first quilts I made was material from Marvin's shirts and Selma's dresses. It was the bonnet girl pattern. This was what we did with things on the homestead, when they were getting beyond use we turned them into other things giving them new life as a blanket, rug, or another piece of clothing.

Later on, with the help of a friend I redid the Bonnet Girl quilt. I removed my original hand tied knots, which had bonded the quilt in beauty, warmth, and love all those early years. My friend used her quilting machine to add scallop stitching. I think it is even more beautiful now. I gave this quilt to Selma because it was she I was thinking about when I made it. She still has it.

Sledding

It was winter, just after the Christmas celebrations. We had a lot of snow that year with high drifts and banks. Bill and Phil had finished their chores and were off playing with some of the neighbor kids from the upper bench. It was a calm sunny day, and I could hear the kid's voices, so I knew they were okay. They came in for lunch and changed into dry clothes. After lunch, they headed back out to join more kids to go sledding. Selma and Bud wanted to join them. I was busy with housework and the younger kids, so I agreed, not thinking too much about it. Of course, the older boys were almost teenagers now and not too thrilled with the idea.

It was wash day. The sun was shining bright and would help dry the diapers and other clothes. I filled the wringer-wash-tub with more clothes but couldn't find the lid. I knew I had it just before lunch but now it was nowhere to be found. To make matters worse Marilyn was crying because she couldn't find her little ironing board. She wanted to help me do laundry with the new little laundry basket, iron, and ironing board that we gave her for Christmas. She loved that little pink ironing board and iron; the little iron got warm enough to press cotton but not hot enough to burn little fingers.

After searching for a while, Marvin disappeared to quiet the crying and solve my laundry problem. He came back with a round wooden lid for the washing machine and a small wooden ironing board for Marilyn. I got the wash done and Marilyn was happy ironing on the board that her daddy made.

Later that evening over supper the boys were asked if they had seen the washer lid and the little ironing board. They swore they had not.

The boys woke early the next morning eager to get their chores done and go back up the hill for more sledding. Selma and Bud wanted to go again, this time the older boys didn't seem to mind as much. Bud disappeared to get his horse. Selma proudly put on the new coat she got for Christmas. Bill and Phil were already outside waiting.

We watched them take off heading in the direction of the wind break and back outbuildings. When they disappeared behind the chicken coop we went back into the house to tend to the day's work. Unbeknownst to us, Bill and Phil had removed the hood off one of the cars parked on the side of the property. The kids figured they could have one big sled to ride on. Bud's horse pulled it to the top of the hill. They got the car hood facing downhill, and all four of them would climb on board. Bill and Phil on each side with the two smaller ones, Selma and Bud, in the middle.

After a few hours Marvin decided to head up the hill and check on the kids. They had made a number of trips down the hill by then. The snow was getting compacted and that hood was traveling farther and faster with each run. As Marvin reached the drainage ditch the kids were flying down the hill. They were screaming, laughing, and holding on tight.

This time the hood-sled went even further, slowing to a stop just at the edge of the drainage ditch. When Marvin got to them, they had just plowed through a barbed wire fence; Selma's new coat was shredded, the others ducked down in time to miss it. Marvin was furious. He gave them all a tongue lashing, especially the two older boys. They should have known better; they were endangering the younger ones. He made Bill and Phil drag that car hood back down the hill, without help from Bud's horse. They were quiet after that. I was just thankful that no one got hurt.

That spring when Marvin was making the rounds with the tractor, he found a mangled little pink ironing board and broken washing machine lid. Once more, Bill and Phil got a tongue lashing, extra chores, and into trouble for lying. *Lesson: Don't tell a lie. Sooner or later, that lie will come back to haunt you.*

Learning to Cook

When Marvin and I got married, I had to learn to cook. As a young girl I didn't spend much time in the kitchen helping my mother or Grandma Emilia cook. When I was young we ate mostly vegetables, but here in Wyoming it was meat and potatoes. I learned to cook and eat that way too. Meat was not just farm-raised but wild game as well. Josephine, bless her heart, was my teacher. It seemed that we boiled everything. Vegetables were boiled to death. Meat was either fried in lard or boiled. I think the only thing that Josephine didn't boil was pies, cakes, and cookies.

One day, Marvin, my beloved husband, asked me to make him a pie. I was still very new at cooking. I wanted to make him a special pie for supper that he would be proud of. I worked hard in the kitchen. In Germany the only pies we had were meat pies. I figured out how to make a crust, filling it with a delicious juicy brown gravy, meat, and vegetables. When Marvin came in for supper, I was beaming at my accomplishment. I served up the pie and we ate all of it, enjoying every bite. When it was time to clean up the dishes Marvin asked me, "Where's the pie?" I looked at him in disbelief, "You just ate it for supper." He looked back at me in disbelief, "I wanted a piece of pie *after* dinner." We stood there looking at each other confused. Then we both laughed. Marvin realized that we only had meat pies in Germany and I realized he wanted me to make a sweet pie. The very next day he taught me how to make a berry pie. And that's how I learned to make pies!

We didn't have refrigeration in those early years in Wyoming, but we did have ice boxes. They were made of wood and insulated so that a block of ice could keep things cold. Ice boxes weren't very big so we either kept our meat at a locker in town, smoked it, or dried it.

We raised most of our own food. Chickens were a main staple of our diet both for eggs and meat. In the spring we would receive a shipment of about one hundred chicks and raise them throughout the summer, four or five months. By fall we had a lot of young cocks to cull; these would become fryers. Marvin and Junior did most of the butchering. The kids and I did the cleaning and plucking. The little ones would just watch. I hated the smell of wet burnt feathers and I didn't like seeing those poor birds flop around without their heads, but it had to be. We would get them ready for cold storage so we would have enough to eat throughout winter. The kids loved the scratchers; we scrubbed the feet clean and fried them. Old hens that weren't laying anymore would be culled and made good stewing chickens. We would make noodles or dumplings to go with the stew; I taught my girls how to make them too.

Over time my cooking skills developed and I got pretty good in the kitchen. The kids still ask for my potato salad. I listened and read every recipe given to me. The butcher advised me on cooking wild game — add oil because it's so lean, increase the spices, and other great tips. The other homesteader wives shared their recipes and secrets. It was a very special time in my life.

Becoming a Citizen

When I married Marvin and we decided to move to the U.S. I knew that I wanted to be the best citizen that I could possibly be. I felt so much gratitude for the troops and the American people who helped lift me out of those darkest of times. I wanted to make my family and husband proud of me. I wanted to be proud of myself.

It's a lot of work to become a U.S. Citizen. It took me seven years. I worked very hard to learn the principles of democracy, system of government, rights, and responsibilities, along with American history. I have to thank Mrs. Charles Nunley who, in the final months, came to the homestead every week and reviewed the lessons with me. I had to learn a lot about our great country to become a part of it. I had picked up the language very quickly, even though I still had trouble with some words. But, I believe most people understood what I was trying to say.

Marvin and Marilyn went with me, along with several of our neighbors. My dear friend Carmen Hirst also stood witness for me at the district court in Basin.

On May 13th 1954 in Basin, Wyoming, I became a naturalized citizen of the United States of America. I can't begin to tell you how honored and proud I felt that day.

Figure 145: Proud Day Receiving my US Citizenship, 1954

Most people born and raised in America have no idea how good we have it. We can vote and have the freedom of speech; when I was a child growing up in Germany, we didn't have that. I was born and raised in a small humble village that would later be surrounded by so much tragedy. My parents sacrificed what little they had to send me to school; high school was not compulsory. That schooling saved my life and paved my way to America. I studied hard to become an American citizen. I am very proud of it

Drowning in Oil

In June of 1955, the homesteaders received our first telephones. Like everything else in homestead life, even such a simple thing like telephone service would start with its own drama.

Mountain States Telephone and Telegraph was installing cables and poles. They had right-of-way down the road and, if needed, onto the property. One morning they were digging trenches for cable about one hundred yards from our house when they broke an underground pipeline. This was a large twelve-inch oil pipeline that belonged to Service Pipeline Company. This was a high-pressure oil pipeline (operating at 500-1500 pounds pressure) pumping oil from the oil fields in the Bad Lands to the refinery in Cody. Oil spouted high into the air for nearly an hour until Service Pipeline was able to close the gates on either side.

The Sheridan Press reported in a June 21st 1955 article, that "The break occurred only about 100 yards from the home of Mr. and Mrs. Marvin Bodle. For a time, the wind blew the geyser-like tower of oil away from the Bodle home. When the wind changed, portions of the oil blew on trees within the Bodle yard. The family was greatly worried that their front yard would be buried by a flood of oil. Men with shovels directed the flow of oil down the road eastward from the Bodle farm home." We were drowning in oil.

Mountain States Telephone made good on everything. All the dirt in our front yard was dug up, hauled off, and replaced with new soil. Allen got a new pair of shoes, clothes, and a stroller because he managed to scoot himself into the oily goo.

Junior left the homestead to us shortly after this and went to work in the oil fields. Hugh also came to live with us in the big house; he was beginning to go blind and needed extra help. The kids, especially Selma, helped their grandfather a lot. Larry was born shortly after.

Lawrence Ray Bodle was born March 3rd, 1956.

Larry had my father's large ears and big smile. He had reddish brown hair and brown eyes, blessing us with another child that looked like me. Larry was named after two of our close neighbors and friends, Lawrence Powers and Ray Siefer. He developed early and grew up fast. Larry was always following his dad or older brothers around. At a very young age Larry was taking things apart and soon learned how to put them back together. He loved puzzles and challenges. Like his older brother Phil, he was a dare devil. Larry had my poor heart racing over one thing or another. He was fearless, yet a real charmer. Girls were always making a fuss over him, even when he was a baby, so his older brothers nicked named him "the chick magnet".

This was also the time that both Allen and Marilyn came down with measles, followed by chickenpox. Measles were very dangerous and would take the lives of many children. Chickenpox wasn't as deadly but it was highly contagious and annoying. Vaccines hadn't been created yet. It was hard to care for the family when everyone was in quarantine. Larry in his crib, Allen and Marilyn in their rooms, and everyone else trying to keep their distance. It was a scary time; life seemed so fragile. Larry and I ended up in the hospital. After everyone got better, Marvin took Larry's crib out and burned it. This was the crib that Marvin made for

Marilyn and was later used for Allen and Larry. He drove to Powell, went to Gambles, and came home with a brand new store-bought crib for Larry. That crib would serve our family as it continued to grow.

We got our first television after Larry was born. It was black and white and we had three, or maybe four channels to watch. In our home, television was not something to turn on whenever you wanted to. It was a special treat. There was a set time for watching television. Marvin would decide what we would watch. Generally, we would watch television in the evening, after supper, after all the chores were done, and after homework was completed.

Homestead Hospitality

School was in Powell, about fourteen miles away. The school bus for our section of the homestead was filled with thirty-five kids, including my five, and would make a roundtrip every school day. One winter when the kids were in school, a severe snow storm whipped up. The school closed early that day so the kids could get home before things got too bad.

The snow was really coming down, the wind was howling, and big snow drifts were building up all around the house. Our house was the third stop on the school bus route; six kids had already been dropped off. It was near blizzard conditions. Carol, the driver, let our five kids off at the house and started up the road to the next stop. A huge drift had built up at the edge of our property between the canal and the drainage ditch on the other side. The driver misjudged the depth of the snow, slid, and the bus got stuck on the edge of the drainage ditch.

The ditch was deep. The drift was high. The wind was driving the snow even harder. It was a white-out. Marvin got out the tractor. I took the kids from the bus into the house and made them hot chocolate while Marvin and Carol worked to pull the bus out of that ditch.

They weren't able to get the bus back on the road, not in these conditions. So, with homestead hospitality, the twenty-four remaining kids along with the bus driver were our guests for the night.

I got ground meat out of the freezer, made Sloppy Joes for dinner, and we had a big slumber party. Marvin had lots of sleeping bags and blankets among his hunting stuff. The kids did their homework, sang songs, and played games until they fell asleep.

We were thankful for the telephone and called all the kids' parents to let them know that their children were safe with us. Larry and Lee Powers, whose children were first off the bus, notified the highway department. By the next morning the storm calmed down. Marvin, Larry, and several other neighbors got the bus pulled out and back on the road. The road department came and cleared the rest of the route. Everyone made it back home safely.

Homestead High-Jinx and Prairie Pranks

Cousin Wayne

One summer cousin Wayne came to spend a couple of weeks with us. Wayne was Junior's stepson, a city kid, born and raised in town. He had never lived in the country and had no clue what it was like to be on the farm. This was the summer that I realized just how ornery Bud could be.

All the kids were working with me in the garden, pulling weeds and picking vegetables. The kids were talking, showing Wayne around, telling him what the plants were, explaining what to pull and what not to pull. Wayne was eager to learn and help. Wayne asked Bud, "What's that?" pointing to a large purple fruit. Bud dutifully replied, "It's an eggplant." Then Wayne asked another simple question, "How do you know when it's ripe?" Without hesitation, Bud looked Wayne right in the eye and responded, "When it cackles." Bud kept a straight face, didn't blink, but couldn't hold it for long before bursting into laughter. Bud just couldn't resist! It took poor Wayne a minute to fully understand that Bud was pulling his leg.

During that same visit, Bud and Wayne were going horseback riding. Bud saddled the horses and gave Wayne instructions on how to get on and off the horse. Wayne was going to be riding Flossie, Bud was on another horse. Wayne got up into the saddle without too much trouble; he was trying to figure out how to get the horse to move, something Bud hadn't bothered to explain yet. When Flossie wouldn't move, Bud said, "Give her a good kick with your heel and say giddy up." Wayne did just that and Flossie took off at full gallop. Now poor Wayne wants her to stop. Finding the humor in Wayne's inexperience, Bud just couldn't resist, yelling out to him, "Push the button." Wayne was terrified, hammering on the saddle horn to no avail. Bud was nearly falling out of his saddle with laughter. Tears were rolling down both of their checks, poor Wayne from fear and mischievous Bud from laughter. When Bud regained his composure, he rode up next to Wayne and told him to pull up on the reins. Flossie stopped immediately. At that point, Wayne had his fill of horses and didn't want to go out for any more rides.

The summer nights were warm. Marvin helped the kids set up a tent in the yard so they could sleep outside. One sunny afternoon the kids asked to go to the swimming hole for a dip. Their favorite swimming spot was at the far end of the field, past the corrals and garden. Of course, I told them it was okay. Selma, Bud, and Wayne took off first with Marilyn and Allen tailing along behind through the alfalfa. They spotted some movement in the field in front of them and decided to investigate. They caught a glimpse of something black, white, and furry.

I do not know who was the instigator, Selma or Bud or maybe both of them, but they told Wayne it was a little black and white kitten. They all went looking for it, telling Wayne that if he caught it, "be sure to put its tail between its legs." Wayne grabbed that little black and white kitten but before he could get that tail between its legs he got sprayed. Selma and Bud got squirted too. What an awful stench. Their eyes were burning too. They turned around and came running back toward the house with the two little ones following behind. Well, that poor baby skunk was just as upset and confused as the kids, running ahead of them spraying as it went before veering off into the alfalfa field.

I heard the screaming, looked up from what I was doing, and could make out the three taller kids running back in my direction. They were frantic but I couldn't hear what they were yelling. Then the smell hit me. I stopped them short of the house. Oh my God, how they stunk. All five of them had gotten sprayed by that little skunk. I had them strip right there.

Marvin drove up right in the middle of all this commotion. He could see and smell what had happened. Marvin got the old wash tub out and grabbed jars of tomato juice. We bathed those kids several times before the smell went away. Yes, the kids got to sleep outside in the tent that night. Frankly, we didn't want them in the house. Marvin buried the clothes and shoes because there was no way to get the smell out. When the story came out about "the kitten thing", Selma and Bud got assigned a few extra farm chores.

I don't know how Wayne put up with his ornery cousins; they always seemed to be trying to pull something over on him and yet he still liked them.

The Fence

Bud was the first boy child blessed to Marvin and me. Even as a little guy he wanted to follow the older boys around. Bill and Phil would often play little tricks on Bud, as kids will do. At the time we had some pigs and a low voltage fence to keep them in their pen. Bill and Phil often forgot that it was electrified, grab the fence, and got shocked.

One morning while the older boys were doing their chores, little Bud was following behind as usual. "Time for some fun with Bud," they thought. I don't know who came up with the idea but they obviously decided it was time to see Bud's reaction when he got "bitten" by the fence. His big brothers told Bud to grab the fence.

Looking up at his brothers, doing as he was told, Bud extended his chubby little hand, and grabbed hold of the wire. Nothing happened. He stood there holding on to the fence and looking up at them. "Let go!" one said. He let go and they told him, "Try over here." He did. Nothing happened.

"Stand back." Something must be wrong with the fence, they thought. Bill and Phil both grabbed ahold of the fence and got shocked. Bud got the big laugh as his brothers got "bitten" by the fence and jumped back with a yelp. The electric fence was "live". What they didn't know was that little Bud was wearing rubber boots. He was not grounded and was never going to get shocked.

.

Snipe Hunting

Bill and Phil brought a friend home from school one day. The friend was more of a "city kid" and didn't know life on the homestead. They told him they were going Snipe hunting. Snipe is a type of wading bird with a long slender bill and plumage that changes to help them blend into their surroundings. They are not easy to spot.

Bill and Phil told their friend that Snipes come out only at night. They drove their friend back into the bad lands, behind the benches. Bill and Phil prepared him with instructions, a flash light, and a bag. They told him that this was a perfect spot to wait, they would flush out some Snipe, and chase them in his direction. He just needed to stay very still and they were sure he would catch one. Bill and Phil took off.

Dinner time rolled around. I asked the boys where their friend from town was? Bill and Phil started laughing. Marvin finally got the story out of them between bursts of laughter. Marvin was not amused. He made Bill and Phil take him out to where they left the young man.

The next day Bill and Phil had extra chores pulling weeds. Marvin happily took the young man hunting.

Grandpa Hugh

Hugh was starting to have more health issues. His eye sight and hearing were not very good. Although we didn't really know it, Hugh had dementia and sometimes would get violent. It was late summer and I was pregnant again, several months along with baby number six. I was sweeping the floor and something set him off. He was a very tall man and still very strong. I don't know if it was the movement or the swishing of the broom across the floor but he jumped up, grabbed me, and started shaking me. The children tried to intervene but he just couldn't be stopped. I was scared for my new baby's life, as well as mine. Bud ran out of the house and lit off across the field towards where his dad was driving the tractor. Marvin bolted back to the house, came in, and stopped it. Hugh was quiet for a long time after that. I think Marvin may have scared him.

It was a difficult pregnancy. I was told to stay off my feet as much as possible. But as a homestead wife with five kids still at home that was not something I did very well.

That winter Marvin went to work in Montana to help get us through the winter. He came home on his days off, weather permitting. Grandpa Hugh had never really gotten used to indoor plumbing and still went outside, feeling his way along the side of the house. Needless to say, this was a problem because he no longer was able to see where he was going and would often get lost. We were worried about his safety so Marvin added a rope, that we called "the grandpa guide" to help him find his way. Wyoming winters were always very demanding. During one of those long lonely weeks when Marvin was in Montana, we had a particularly severe snow storm. Selma was busy with the baby and I was helping Bud with school work when Marilyn shouted that the back door was open. It was dark, the wind was howling, and snow was piling up against the house. Worst of all, Hugh was missing.

We called out for him but got no response. What was I going to do? I couldn't go out and leave the kids. What if something happened to me? I picked up the telephone, called Jack Hirst, asked if he would brave the weather, and come help me find Hugh. He said he would. I was worried and, in the meantime, bundled up Bud to go out and look for Grandpa Hugh. The wind was blowing so hard that I tied a rope around his waist so I wouldn't lose him too.

I sent Bud out the back door to look for Grandpa Hugh. Bud inched his way along the grandpa guide and did find Hugh, face down, buried in snow. Jack arrived in time to help us get Hugh back into the house. Hugh had a heart attack. We called the doctor who walked Jack and me through what to do to help him. Jack stayed until the storm let up. Once the roads were passable, the doctor drove out to the homestead to check on Hugh and me.

By the beginning of October, I was having more pain and spotting heavily. The baby didn't seem to be moving much and I still had a week to go. Marvin took me to see the doctor who sent me straight to the hospital. The doctor said the baby was having some problems and that he would deliver the baby via cesarean section. He said it was important to do it immediately or there was a possibility that neither of us would make it. Marvin and I were both scared. Marvin called the neighbors asking them to take the kids for the night and someone stayed with Hugh.

I don't remember much about the delivery, I was in a lot of pain, and they gave me something for it. Robbin was delivered by C-section. When I woke up, we had a beautiful little boy. The doctor said we were both very lucky, the umbilical cord had wrapped around his neck when he turned toward the birth canal. We were both in the hospital for several days, longer than I was with any of the other kids. He had a few problems in the first few months but grew into a healthy baby. I was slow to heal and ordered not to lift anything heavy. Selma helped out a lot and took care of Robbin every day when she got home from school.

Robbin Karl Bodle was born October 3rd 1959 in the fall of that year. We were now a family of ten.

Robbin was a name that Marvin and I both chose. We didn't know if the baby would be a boy or a girl, we just liked the name, and it would fit either a boy or a girl. Karl was my father's name, which we added after he was born. He had reddish hair and big brown eyes.

Figure 15: Our Family of Ten, 1960

Hugh was confined to bed and I was still healing from the C-section. I turned and cleaned Hugh as best I could. My incision was not fully healed, it was tearing and it was painful. The doctor contacted the county nurse who started looking for a home that could help care for Hugh. Hugh had only ever worked on the farm and had never paid into the social security system. He didn't have any money but somehow the county nurse figured out how to help him. Hugh didn't go without putting up a fight. They say he knocked down two male nurses trying to get him into a room. *When we moved into town four years later, in 1963. We got to visit Hugh more often.*

Bill was in a serious truck accident, broke his back, and spent time in the big hospital in Billings, Montana. By the time Bill healed up, he was ready to leave for college. The same summer Phil went to work on a ranch after his last year in high school. Thankfully we had telephone service to the house now that our family was spreading it wings. The phone helped keep us connected as the older boys headed off on their own.

Hunting, Fishing and Knowing the Land

We spent thirteen years on the homestead. It was a great time in our lives but not without its challenges and funny stories. Many things happened on our homestead. I know that some of these stories are a bit out of order, but wanted to share them with you as they pop into my head.

After a few difficult winters where there wasn't quite enough food to get through the entire winter, it was obvious to us that we needed more than just the crops we raised. Marvin loved to hunt. He hunted with respect. Hunting with respect means that you never killed something unless you were going to eat it or it was going to hurt someone.

On most Sundays after church service, the men would gather and talk. One Sunday late in the summer a member of the church, Cie Rogers, mentioned that he was in need of more hunting guides and horses. Cie had several groups of hunters coming in from out of state and could use some help. Marvin thought about this. We had twelve horses now and we could certainly use some extra meat for the winter. The guide work would be just after the harvest and there would be a little extra money in it too. Marvin said "Yes", got his Wyoming Guide License, and was soon set up to lead a group of three hunters.

The group had three men from California, an IBM executive, a Dodge dealer, and one other man. The men had a great time. After that, every year the same group of men would return requesting that Marvin guide them on a hunt. He became friends with Del Heath and Hanson Murray from Los Gatos, California.

Marvin guided other groups too. One group was organized by a dentist, Doc Uhl from Hamilton, Ohio who enjoyed big game hunting. The dentist would bring his wife with him from time to time. She stayed in Cody while the men went hunting. I enjoyed it when Doc brought his wife with him. During the day she would spend time with me and the kids on the homestead before driving back to Cody for the night. She always brought something for the kids to play with or to make. On one trip she brought yarn dolls for the girls to put together and little wooden trucks for the boys to build and paint. She would sit with them and help them. They had no children of their own and she enjoyed her time with them. Marilyn fondly remembers the little brown Indian doll that Doc's wife helped her make.

On a trip to Montana we got caught in a massive traffic jam. This wasn't your typical traffic jam and I had never seen anything like it. We came over a hill and in front us were thousands of buffalo, or so it seemed. It was a huge herd, the biggest I have ever seen. They took up the entire road. We couldn't pass; we could barely move. We inched our way forward but they clearly had no interest in moving out of our way. It really was the funniest thing I had ever seen. It took us almost an hour to go the fifteen-minute drive down to the Madison River, the herd moved so slowly. As we neared the Madison River, the herd joined up with another even larger herd. The Madison River flows down out of Wyoming through Yellowstone, into Montana. It contains some of the most amazing wildlife I have ever seen: black and grizzly bear, elk, moose, and the most beautiful swans and cranes.

In addition to the wildlife, the area where we lived was immersed in Indian history. Near us was the Crow Tribe in Sheridan, Cherokee in Powell, Plains Indians in Cody, and the Arapahoe Tribe further south, near Riverton. On the

116

lower bench was an old stage stop that still had an arrow sticking out of the building above the door by a second story window. There were teepee rings scattered along Eagles Nest Creek where the tribes spent time and on the upper bench near us. We knew about Pow Wows, but white men were not allowed in because they were spiritual events. I really didn't know any of the Indians very well, they didn't mingle much with the white folks. They seemed to me to be just like the rest of the people. From the many stories I had been told, I admired them for knowing how to survive off the land and not waste anything. I think it is sad that we took the land from them. What America did to the Indians seemed much the same as what happened to my family and neighbors in my homeland. The parallel to Nazi Germany and Russian occupation seemed undeniable, to me.

My Hunting Story

I have my own hunting story, too. I would also act as a hunting guide for day trips when needed, taking men out to hunt on the Belknap Ranch above Cody. But that's not the story I need to tell you.

My hunting story actually took place just before we moved to the homestead. It was on a hunting trip with Marvin and our dear friends, Ken and Shirley Bates, in the fall of 1949. On this hunt I killed my first bull elk. I was a short distance from the others in the group when I saw this huge bull elk. I laid on the ground to steady myself and placed six shots in that bull elk, all within an area the size of my palm. That trusted Winchester .25-35 brought the elk down on the spot. I was so proud of that kill and wanted those horns but Marvin didn't feel the same. He said there was no room for the horses to pack both the meat and the horns out, so he said the horns would have to stay behind. I agreed that the 300+ pounds of meat were the most important.

But, I wanted those horns.

117

I wanted them so badly that I carried them out of the back country on my shoulders. Marvin proudly displayed the horns of his kills and I wanted to add my own six-point rack to the collection. The trip was nearly twelve miles. These horns stood almost as tall as I was. When we got to a river crossing, Marvin thought that surely I would give up. Ken and Shirley felt bad for me but didn't want to anger Marvin. They still wanted to help me, so Ken tied the elk horns to his saddle horn and dragged them to the other side. Marvin hoisted me up on the back of his horse and took me across the river, chewing me out the whole way across for wanting those stupid horns. On the other side of the river I resumed walking with my precious horns on my shoulders. By the time we got back to the trucks my shoulders were sore, raw, and bleeding. But I got my point across and I got those elk horns.

My story got told and retold. I never really understood why. I was told that I became something of a hero to Wyoming women and "a 4'10" 100-pound legend" among the men. The CSA (Christian Sportsman Association) even wrote up the story a number of years later in the magazine, *Power*. Here's an excerpt from John Riden's article, "On the Trail of Big Game", published in November 1958.

> Men of the CSA are an adventurous lot - and so are the wives who accompany their husbands. Seasoned hunters like to tell the story of Hannah Bodle, a little Germany war bride who, though she had driven an ambulance in World War II and been wounded, found elk hunting an adventure in a class by itself, both she and her husband, Marvin, are CSA members.
>
> On a hunt together, they camped at the base of a mountain. Early the next morning they heard a bull elk bugling above them and hurriedly set out after him, with Marvin anxiously leading the way by some distance.

Figure 6: My Prized Six Point Elk Horns

Back row: Junior & Marvin
Front row: Phil, me, and Bill with Bud & Selma holding the horns

Stopping momentarily to rest, Hannah saw through a clearing just to her right a form that looked to her to be almost as big as an elephant. Partially veiled in mist, it was the bull elk.

Quickly 100-pound Hannah leveled her gun and fired. Infuriated, the elk charged, and she shot again, courageously holding her ground. But on came the elk, downhill toward the small woman. Finally, after her third shot, the maddened beast collapsed.

Simultaneously her husband arrived on the scene, his eyes bulging. Examination showed that Mrs. Bodle had placed the three shots within a small area, any one of which would have eventually killed the elk.

Homestead Holidays and Wyoming Weather

Holidays were always special. When the kids were little, holidays had magic to them and we truly enjoyed them. In today's world they don't seem to be as special anymore, I'm not sure why. But each holiday and season had a special charm of their own on the homestead.

Spring

For Valentine's Day we made cards and hearts. They would be all over the house. The kids exchanged them with their special friends.

Easter Sunday was a big event at our church. I loved making the girls a special new dress. Marvin would get each of us girls a new hat and pair of gloves. I would sew new shirts for the boys. I loved it when I could make matching shirts, if there was enough fabric from feed sacks, a full skirt, or some clothes that had been passed down to us. We gathered up eggs, hard boiled, and dyed them. The kids got so excited. We would sit around the kitchen table and dye them using food coloring and beet juice. Marvin and Junior would hide the eggs. As the kids got older, the older ones would hide them. We would often find those eggs later in the year when working in the yard, raking, or gardening. If we could afford it, we might add a store-bought candy bunny to the basket. There would be a pot luck lunch at the church with games and another egg hunt for the kids.

Summer

Even though school was out, June Bible Studies would have the kids back on the bus into Powell, if they weren't needed to help in the fields. We loved all the picnics. There would be a big church picnic. The 4-H would have a picnic on the river up in the mountains. One year on our way to the 4-H picnic, just past Cody near the Buffalo Bill Reservoir, we drove through a swarm of bees. In the back of the truck, the kids ended up with honey and bees all over them; thank goodness no one was badly stung.

The 4-H was a big part of homesteading life. It is a network of youth organizations with the mission to help young people reach their fullest potential (www.4-H.org). The four "Hs" stand for the four areas of development: head, heart, hands, and health. Our older children, Bill, Phil, Selma, Bud, and Marilyn, were all active in 4-H and I became a 4-H Leader. To become a 4-H Leader, I had to go to Laramie, Wyoming, along with several other homesteaders who wanted to be leaders. We took special leadership classes at the university. I also learned more about sewing, becoming a certified 4-H Leader in sewing. Others became leaders in cooking, canning, gardening, or livestock raising. It was a wonderful way to pass down life-skills to the children. Each year the kids would show off the results of their work at the Park County Fair, in competition or on display.

Summer was time for watermelon challenges. Marvin cut the watermelon length wise, the kids sat around the picnic table eating and spitting seeds. A favorite challenge was to see who could spit the seeds the farthest. We enjoyed barbequing outside. There was always fresh roasted corn-on-the-cob and marshmallows to toast. The older kids would play hide-and-seek in the yard until well after dark. Sometimes we spread a blanket out on the lawn and would gaze up into the night skies telling stories, watching the clouds dance, and looking for shooting stars.

Figure 17: Funny Looking Horse!

Friends from town often came out for a late afternoon barbeque. The kids were always making up games. Sometimes we couldn't figure out just what they were doing but they were having fun with horse apple throwing contests, pig lasso tournaments, sheep rodeos, or king of the manure pile. They seemed to be able to turn anything into a game. The homestead held pleasures that the kids from town did not get to enjoy very often like swimming in the shallow water of the canal, horseback riding, lassoing the baby pigs, or riding on the sheep.

Fourth of July was a big celebration; there was a parade in Powell or Cody with fireworks after. Everyone loved the fireworks, except me. The loud noise reminded me of war and I just couldn't get used to it. Fireworks had their dangers too, and I worried that the kids could get hurt. Fortunately, mine didn't but a lot of other neighbors weren't as lucky. One lost some fingers, another lost his eyesight, and another went deaf. Little hands were never safe around sparklers and fireworks. One fourth of July it even snowed on us. We were in Powell for the fireworks, all prepared to picnic and enjoy the show. It snowed! Not much, but it snowed! I loved celebrating Independence Day; it had special meaning for me. I loved the barbeques and getting together with our friends and neighbors. These wonderful times left me with truly great memories.

Summer was often hot and muggy. Late afternoon thunderstorms were common, rolling in across the high plains. I didn't like these storms. They were a dark reminder from my childhood of how unpredictable the lightning can be. As a young girl in Jaentsdorf a late afternoon summer thunderstorm rolled in. Our neighbor and her twin children were working in the field. She didn't stop work right away, thinking the storm would move away from them. Realizing the storm was heading toward them, she finally stopped work, slung the hoe on her shoulder, and headed toward the village with the kids on each side. They had not gone far when the sky lit up with lightning and thunder roared. The lightning struck the hoe and our neighbor, throwing the two kids in opposite directions. Several of the villagers saw the whole thing; it all happened so fast that there was nothing anyone could do for the poor woman. The children ended up okay, but it left a lasting impression on everyone.

Our kids didn't like thunderstorms either; maybe I had something to do with that. The kids would run and hide with the sound of thunder or when the sky lit up. If a storm came during the night they somehow found their way into our bed. There could be six of us in that little double bed. When the kids fell back to sleep, Marvin and I would carry them back to their beds. Marvin would tell them, "Don't worry; it is only a potato wagon rumbling by."

One storm brought hail the size of golf balls. It destroyed an entire crop of beans and grain, leaving dents in cars, trucks, and metal roofs. There's no way to recoup after something like that happens in the late summer. You're out all that hard work and money. It hurts.

Fall

Fall was very busy. The harvest consumed all of our time and energy. I had to get the kids off to school with books, lunch boxes, and homework in hand. It was my final push to get the canning done. Fall reminded me of Jaentsdorf when I was young; it was the same for my parents – harvest, school, and canning. Life somehow was not that much different, here and there.

Halloween was greeted by carved pumpkins on the step by the front door. The number of carved pumpkins grew over the years to eight, one for each of our children. A ghost, made from a sheet, would watch over the house hanging from a tree.

Both kids and parents liked Halloween. The homesteaders got together and made plans for a route for the children. Each area had assigned stops, with the last stop being the 4-H club house for a party. Our 4-H group had a large club house. It was a perfect gathering place for all the homesteaders and their families. The kids were all dressed up in outfits. All of the costumes were home-made; no one bought costumes. I am not sure there even were store-bought costumes at that time. We loaded all the hobos, clowns, and cowboys into a wagon pulled by tractor and took the kids from homestead to homestead. The homesteads were pretty far apart, so the hayride was a big part of the fun. All of the treats were home-made: candy, cookies, caramel apples, popcorn balls, and hot cider. After the hayrides made their rounds, they would come back to the club house for games and more food. It was great fun.

Thanksgiving was a big holiday. A lot of work would go into making the meal a very special one. The kids decorated the house for celebration of the harvest. They made things at school or at home. At Thanksgiving there would be hand-print turkeys, pilgrims, and pumpkins. If Marilyn could find them, there would be pine cone creatures that she and Selma would make.

Winter

One Christmas the kids made Christmas trees from old catalogs and Reader's Digest magazines. Marvin helped to spray paint them, then the kids sprinkled on glitter and decorated them for the table. I never knew what the kids would come up with next. *I still get those surprises today from my kids, grandkids, or greats. I love seeing the creativity and imagination in the things they make. It makes me feel so grateful that these kids are mine and that I was able to help them see the possibilities in unusual things like rocks, clouds, pinecones, and even catalogs.*

Winters were very cold but still beautiful. I loved to sit by the big front window and watch the giant snowflakes falling softly down out of the dark gray skies onto the lawn.

If it wasn't snowing too hard and the wind was calm we would bundle up the kids and send them out to play. Quite often Marvin and I would join them for a while. It was especially fun to make first tracks in new snow and to see who could make the best snow angel. After a storm the kids hurried out to build snowmen, tunnel into the drifts and bombard each other with snow balls. Marvin especially enjoyed the snowball fights with the kids. The little ones would have to run in close to make a hit and always seemed to get a soft snowball in the back before getting away. Their laughter still rings in my memories. Rosy cheeks. Runny noses. Cold little hands.

I can still hear the crunch of snow under our feet as we trudged out to take care of the livestock and the sparkle of the snow in the sun. Long blueish icicles hung down from the eaves of the house and on telephone lines running overhead across the yard. Some nights the sky was so clear and bright that the light from the moon and stars would cast long shadows and reflect off the snow. It seemed like daylight. One night I got to see the northern lights, the aurora borealis. WOW! How beautiful and colorful. I was awestruck. It was one of the most beautiful things I have ever seen.

A Hill of Beans

In the fall of 1962, everything was looking good. We had already taken several loads of beans to town. The rest of the crop was on the ground waiting to be thrashed and loaded. Marvin expected to get this done the next morning then take a hunting party up into the mountains. Everything was ready for both.

Mother nature had other plans.

Early in the morning the wind began to blow. At first, it wasn't so bad, but just before dawn it began to howl. It's what we called a northerner, where the weather comes down from the north. It was relentless. Marvin was up and pacing. We depended on that crop of beans lying in the field to pay back the money we borrowed for seed. The extra money it would bring was needed to help us get through the winter. The wind kept up. The gusts were 30 or 40 miles per hour or more.

At first daylight, Marvin and I made our way out to the field. The wind was still blowing but not quite so hard. As we stood there braced against the wind, we saw the beans scattered like snow across the field. The dried bushes were long gone like tumbleweeds blown against the fence. Marvin was frozen like a statue, I had never seen him like this before. It was as if the wind had blown the spirit out of him. Everything in him seemed to be gone; his spirit shattered. All he could say was, "It's over. What am I going to do?"

The men who came for the hunt were standing beside him. The hunters were that same group of three men from California that came every year. We all just stood there, staring in solemn disbelief.

After breakfast and some coffee Marvin pulled himself back together. He accepted the situation, saying there was nothing he could do about the beans and he had men waiting to go hunting who had already paid for their trip. So, without further ado, he put on his coat and went out to finish loading the horses for the hunting trip. They left for the mountains.

We weren't the only ones to lose our crops that day. The kids and I tried to salvage as much as we could. But we couldn't get a good price for the beans because of all the dirt. One of the neighbors had finished harvesting his potato crop; he let us go into his field and take what we wanted of the remaining potatoes on the ground. Along with some of the beans that we had managed to salvage, the potatoes were a big help. If Marvin got an elk on the hunt, the hunters usually left some meat behind for us. I kept telling myself that we would be okay.

Marvin returned home two weeks later from the hunting party. He was in a better frame of mind. While out on the hunt the guys had long talks about what could be done and other options that we had. Del Heath and Hanson Murray told Marvin to come to California and they would help him find work. They felt that there were lots of opportunities for a guy with Marvin's skills to find employment.

We talked long and hard about the options and about California. In December we asked a neighbor to take the older kids for two weeks. Marvin, Robbin, and I piled into the old GMC truck and headed to California to see if it would work for us.

We drove through Utah and Nevada. The land was barren, even more stark than Wyoming. At times the wind and snow blew hard. The closer we got to California the prettier it got. California was lush by comparison and Los Gatos was like a piece of heaven. There were so many trees and flowers. I got to pick my first oranges. They were unbelievably sweet. We stayed with Hanson and June Murray, visiting with Del and Pat Heath while we were there. I liked California. Marvin got the promise of a job.

Now we had to figure out the challenge of how to make the move. Telling the rest of the family would not be easy either. We would probably have to sell everything, then hope for the best.

We said our goodbyes and were handed a huge box of oranges to eat on the way home. We arrived back home just before Christmas. After the excitement of returning home died down, we told the kids the news. Bud and Selma had mixed feelings. The younger ones thought we were moving to Disneyland; that was all they knew about California. For me, it was another whole new world.

Things happen quickly. Everything fell into place as God answered all of our prayers. The bank found a buyer for the farm in no time. We gave lots of things away and had an auction to sell off everything else that we didn't need; we could only carry so much. We sold everything — dishes, furniture, farm equipment, tools, livestock, chickens, and even some clothes. Each child was allowed one box of toys. Folks came from miles around to the auction. The weather was with us and we were able to make good money. The money was used to settle our debt to the bank, buy a new station wagon, and tuck some money away for the months ahead, when Marvin would be gone. We hoped to even have enough for a down payment on a home in California.

By February of 1963 we found a house to rent in Powell so the kids could finish the school year. We settled into the temporary Powell home and Marvin headed to California to work. Those were lonely times for me. I missed him not being there. The kids kept me busy and were always getting into something. Marvin called at least once a week and every few weeks he would drive up for a quick visit. He told us stories of California. He was looking for a house for us, but hadn't found one yet.

I pinched pennies to make every cent count and to hold on to our savings in hope that we could buy a home. We had some great neighbors. They helped us in lots of ways, big and small. One neighbor shared her coupons with me and others checked in to make sure we were doing okay. Our house in Powell was across the alley from a bakery. The kids would sometimes go to the bakery and get day-old pastries to eat. When the owner found out, he put a few fresh ones out for them and they would usually do something nice in return. To save money I bought the two-day old bread; the kids ate it before it had time to go stale. One thing the kids never quite got used to was powdered milk; they were used to farm fresh milk but that was too expensive in Powell.

When things were quiet and the older kids were off to school, I would walk the little ones around the central part of town. A special pleasure was visiting my friend, Mrs. Mickie, and helping her prepare flower orders at her flower shop. On Sundays it was a short walk down the street for church services and on nice days over to the city park. Bill was living off Avenue E, on one of the Decker farms. Bill married Scarlet Decker and blessed us with two grandchildren. We would get together with them and the kids and grandkids would enjoy playing together. By this time Phil was also married. Phil joined the Air Force out of high school and married Bobby Joe Boyle. He married her when he was home on leave.

Marvin came home in early summer and announced that he found us a house in California. He said we would move in August. The church gave us a farewell party. We loaded what little we had into the back of the old GMC truck. Extra stuff was tied to the roof of the station wagon. We spent our final night in Wyoming at Bill and Scarlet's. After breakfast we loaded the kids and Blackie, the cocker spaniel, into the station wagon.

On August 13th we headed down the road toward a whole new beginning, leaving behind friends, family, and the only life we had known as a family.

Reuniting with Family

Today's youth think that they created social networking, but this was networking at its very best! Without the aid of technology, family and friends looked out for each other and stayed connected.

Thanks to my network of friends, I learned about my family's whereabouts in 1947, just before Selma was born. If it hadn't been for Sofie and Vera's continued search, I may never have found them. Mail took a long time, from a couple of weeks to a couple of months for a letter to get there and back.

I had not seen or heard of my family for five years, from 1942 to 1947. There was a deep inner loneliness and sense of loss in those years. I dearly loved my new family and my new American home, but I was without my roots.

A wall had been built down the middle of Germany and through the city of Berlin, splitting the country into East and West. The Berlin Wall was constructed by the GDR (German Democratic Republic or East Germany) in 1961. It completely cut off the two sides of the country. The wall included guard towers placed along large concrete walls, anti-vehicle trenches, a limited number of control gates and other defenses. A five-mile wide no-mans-land divided East and West Germany with very few checkpoints where people were allowed to cross. Land mines filled no-mans-land and barbed wired surrounded it. People could not freely cross between East and West, if at all.

My youngest brother, Adolf, came to visit a few times. His first visit was around 1966 or 1967, more than twenty years after I left Germany. His merchant marine ship would dock in San Francisco or Stockton and he was able to take leave to visit us. He was the first member of my family that I got to see or touch. It was incredibly special for me after so many years of separation. The kids seemed to love him, even though they could not understand him. I felt a little guilty about the language barrier; I had not taught my children to speak German, I never dreamed I would ever set foot in my homeland again.

Letters from Home

Thanks to the letters from my mother I learned that she had resettled the family in Wolfersdorf, with the help of my Uncle Mo and Aunt Ema, papa's sister. Uncle Mo never gave up and continued to check the Red Cross posters every day for friends and family. He did not give up hope that other friends or family might have survived. One day he came home all excited, having word that Karl, my father, was alive and heading their way.

After papa was taken by the German Gestapo he was put into prison for two years. Later the Nazis sent him to the front lines to fight as a soldier for the country he had been bad mouthing. The Nazis sent prisoners to war with little or no training viewing them as expendable in their war efforts. Papa would never talk about his years in prison or at the front lines. He just said that it was a difficult and painful time for him. I know he also must have been very worried about mother and the kids.

Mother also spoke very little of the war years or the time in the refugee camp. This was a dreadful time in mother's life. She said that it filled her heart with such sadness and pain; she would rather not recall it and was just thankful that they made it out together. Saying only, "Each makes the best and does the best they can." I learned of the story of Erica Wallstein, the Burgermeister's daughter, and my mother finding her in the barn from Erica herself, many years after mother passed away, at one of the village reunions.

Once papa and mother were reunited, they had to decide what to do next. They knew that they could not return to their beloved Jaentsdorf, as the area had been seized by the Poles and Russians. Uncle Mo heard that land surrounding Wolfersdorf was to be divided up among the people. It was a vast land holding that had belonged to a Baron that died in the war.

There was very little, if anything, left of the estate after the ravages of war. Papa and mother decided to stay, determined to start a new life. With material salvaged from the destroyed buildings and other structures, a number of people displaced by the war slowly settled in, rebuilding their lives, starting over again.

Papa built mother a new house, over time, adding some out-buildings, a large garden, and fruit trees. This new home was two stories with an earthen block base over a foot thick. The large upstairs had separate bedrooms for the girls and boys. There was even a cellar for storing canned goods and an attic where mother could dry her herbs. There was running cold water to both floors and "indoor plumbing": the outhouse was inside by the back door. Papa built mother a beautiful sun room, it was a warm spot for her winter flowers. The house and barn were one large structure. The barn section had a hayloft at one end, a work shop at the other, and the milking room in the middle.

Figure 18: House Karl built for Selma in Wolfersdorf after the War

Papa raised livestock, grew willows, and rediscovered his carpentry skills. Papa would weave the willow branches into baskets to sell at the market. Mother had managed to save a few of papa's carpentry tools from Jaentsdorf which encouraged him to do the carpentry work he so loved. Mother's skills in the garden and as an herbalist proved useful too. To rebuild their lives much was done in-trade for other skills, neighbors helping neighbors. Soon a thriving community was coming together. The combination of different skills and cultures began to thrive as one.

Papa was still a feisty little man; the war didn't take that from him. He learned to graft fruit trees in his sixties and continued doing tree work well until the year before he died.

My brothers and sisters grew up in Wolfersdorf, calling it home. Only the two oldest children, Gerda and Arnold, remembered Jaentsdorf.

Gerda grew up to be a beautiful woman despite what she had been through. Her hair was golden blonde and she had bright blue eyes. Gerda was tall and strong. Because of what she went through during the war, she was stronger than rest. She met her husband, Heinz Schneider, while at school. We called him "Big Heinz". Gerda and Big Heinz had three children and five grandchildren.

Arnold never fully recovered from having his legs broken at the refugee camp. As a result, he never grew to be very tall. Because there was no real medical care in the refugee camp, his legs were not set quite right. Many years later in Nuremberg they tried to fix the problem with his legs but that in turn caused him great back pain. He was a fighter and never stopped trying to do whatever he could and then some. Arnold and his wife Elfrieda had four children and five grandchildren.

Renate, like the other two girls, had blonde hair and blue eyes like papa. She was taller than me, but not the tallest. Renate was a gentle soul, much like Arnold and mother. Renate went on to study music and became a kindergarten teacher. Like Grandma Emilia, she was wonderful with kids, especially the little ones. Renate married Heinz Hesse, who became known as "Little Heinz" in the family. They had two children and five grandchildren.

Adolf is my youngest brother and the tallest member of the family. He has the dark hair and eyes of mother, like Arnold and me. After the war, Adolf was a tremendous help to my father in the fields and the garden. Adolf joined the Merchant Marines after escaping the Russian military draft. He had a twenty-year career with the Merchant Marines then settled back in Germany, marrying Ellen. Adolf and Ellen did not have any children.

Erna was so young when I left home that I hardly knew her. I know from mother's letters that she had a lot of health problems and was probably coddled more than the rest of the kids. She survived the blood transfusion administered by the Nazi doctors as a small child. Erna grew up to be a real beauty. Like her sisters, she had blonde hair and blue eyes. Erna and Hermann married, having two children and three grandchildren.

Figure 197: Kurtz Family Reunion, 1976

Erna, Karl, Selma, Adolf, me, Gerda, Renate, and Arnold

I am so thankful that all my family survived the war. It was a blessing to be able to see them and get to know them.

Later, survivor meetings were organized for our village of Jaentsdorf and people began to piece together more of what happened. The survivor meetings were held annually for about ten years. As more stories emerged it was clear that no one walked away without some tragedy. War is hell on the people who live through it.

My First Trip to Germany

By 1969 it had been nearly twenty-five years since I had been in Germany. I received word that my father would be undergoing stomach surgery. It was a tough time for me because we knew that he might not make it. I waited anxiously for each letter, praying it would be good news.

Mother wrote and said the surgery went well. The next letter would not be so optimistic and so it went back and forth. He had a terrible stomach and would have part of it removed and replaced with the stomach of a goat. Well, that is what I heard but I am not entirely sure that was true or if they were telling me that papa was "a tough old goat". He was having trouble. Mother was worried that he wouldn't make it. She wished they could see the kids and meet Marvin.

Marvin worked at Stanford University and had a colleague who was from Germany with family on both sides, East and West. He told Marvin that it was possible to obtain a special Visa to be able to make the trip into East Germany to visit with my family. It was now early 1970 and Marvin put everything into action to make this trip happen for me. He arranged to get the special Visas, passports, plane tickets, and four weeks off work. It was a tall order.

Mother's last letter said papa was failing. Marvin told me that he had been working on making all the arrangements. I was elated. I quickly sat down and wrote my mother with tears of joy in my eyes. I told her all about the special Visas that would allow us to pass through the Berlin Wall, that Marvin was working on everything, and we would be there as soon as we could, possibly July. I would send the exact dates later when all the details came together. Marvin said we would take the two youngest children with us, Larry and Robbin. By April, everything was in order. Now, according to mother, papa was doing remarkably well with word that we were coming to visit.

Originally, Marilyn was not going to join us on the trip because she was working. In May, she learned that she wouldn't get a job she was hoping for and we wanted her to join us too. It was now only seven weeks before we would be leaving. The time was tight to get the passport and Visa, but we started the process the very next day. Marvin was able to get another ticket. Now we had to wait for the passport and Visa to arrive. We waited. We checked the mailbox every day, still no passport and no Visa. The day before departure Marilyn's passport finally arrived, but no Visa. What would we do without the Visa? Marvin said we'll just have to figure it out when we get there. The Department of State said her Visa had been approved.

The next morning with all our bags packed, airline tickets in hand, passports and Visas in place, minus one, we headed to the San Francisco Airport. Airports and air travel were different in the 1970s. Friends and family could sit with you in the gate area or meet an incoming flight. People were allowed to smoke in the terminal and on the airplanes. A man next to me in the gate area was smoking a big huge smelly cigar. I was happy when they finally allowed us to board the plane so I could get away from him.

Everyone boarded and were in their seats. After what seemed like a long time sitting on the plane, the pilot announced, "We are on hold, waiting for a special delivery. It shouldn't be much longer, and we will be able to depart."

A few more minutes went by, then a uniformed man entered the plane. He looked very authoritative, definitely in a position of importance. He spoke quietly to the stewardess, she pointed down the aisle in our direction. Everyone was watching him, wondering what this special delivery was, as he walked down the aisle with some sort of official-looking bag in hand.

He stopped short of our row, and asked, "Is there a Marilyn Bodle present?" We were all bewildered. I believe Marilyn thought they were going to take her off the plane. I could see the fear in her eyes as she said, "Yes, I am Marilyn Bodle."

The man held out his hand, introduced himself, explaining that he was from the immigration office, and had been sent to deliver her Visa. He reached into his bag, pulled out the official paperwork, and placed it in Marilyn's trembling hand. He seemed to take great pride in his special delivery, then in strong gentle sounding voice said, "Miss Bodle, have a safe trip. Good luck. We hope your grandfather is doing well." He turned, thanked the stewardess, and left the plane. It was amazing! I doubt that anything like that would happen today.

It was a long trip. We changed planes in Chicago and again in Frankfurt, Germany, to a smaller plane that took us to Nuremberg. We spent the night, taking a train the next morning to Hof before crossing into East Germany. Hof is located on the banks of the Saale River in the northeastern corner of Bavaria at the Czech Border.

Talking with people on the train to Hof about our trip, we were warned to be very careful, that the Russian guards would use any excuse to detain someone. I did my best to translate this information to the family. My German was very rusty, I hadn't spoken my native language in years, and at first it didn't come back as quickly as I hoped. I had to translate in my mind, thinking through each word in both languages.

We got off the train at Hof and went to have breakfast. Marilyn was fascinated with the pretty glass teapot and cup that they served her tea in. The waiter told us that it was Jena Glass and came from East Germany, not far from where we were heading. The waiter also left us with more solemn words of caution.

We boarded the train heading east. It was sunny with a few puffy clouds in the sky, but as we traveled further into Eastern Germany, the sky grew grayer. The train came to a stop. Then after a few minutes, it started moving again. The people stopped talking as much, and only in low tones. Then the train came to a complete stop, and it got deadly quiet.

Two young soldiers armed to the hilt came into our compartment, they walked over to Marilyn and started asking her questions. Of course, she couldn't understand them so I did my best to grasp what they were saying and answer their questions. We handed over our passports and Visas. After a few minutes the compartment door opened and the scariest person I had ever seen stepped in. She took one look at us, and yelled something at the two young soldiers in Russian. They left so fast it made our heads spin, leaving us behind with this scary woman and her ugly dog.

She was in full uniform with an ammunition belt across her chest, a rifle with bayonet in hand, and her ugly dog with a spiked collar at her side. She was the most frightening person I have ever seen, and I'm sure my family felt the same way. She turned to Marilyn and began questioning her. Marilyn's eyes were as big as saucers.

When I got my wits back, I tried to politely explain that other than my rusty German, no one in our group spoke Russian or German. This seemed to anger her even more. I remembered the warnings we had received and prayed that Marvin would not intervene. At last, she seemed to calm down some. She went through all of our belongings taking whatever she wanted — coffee, chocolate, and soft toilet paper for my mother, sweet smelling soap for my sisters, my new shoes, and more. We must have been the last ones to be inspected because shortly after she left our compartment, taking all our stuff with her, the train jolted forward and we were on our way again.

Other people on the train hadn't spoken to us very much but after this inspection stop they came to see if we were okay. They said we were now leaving no-mans-land, that five-mile-wide strip of land filled with landmines and barb wire that separated East and West Germany. It stretched the full length of Germany, dividing it in two. Very few Americans traveled through this area which, we think, is why she was so rough on us.

We had to check in with officials in every town we planned to visit. We were required to pay the government a fee for each day or spend a certain amount of money while we were there. Everywhere we went there were large bill boards about Vietnam and the bad Americans.

The trains went everywhere. We changed trains several times and I got mixed up on the last stop. We were supposed to meet my family in Berga. I didn't know there were two train stops in Berga, we got off at the first stop but should have gone to the second stop. It didn't take long for the people to figure out who we were with all our suitcases. My sister, Gerda, lived near the first train stop. In this small close-knit community, many of the townsfolk knew we were coming. Word traveled quickly to the next station where my family was waiting "that the Americans had arrived." It all worked out. The townsfolk took care of us, serving us ice cream while we waited.

This was a very emotional time for me. I will always remember seeing the faces of my parents after more than twenty-five years. I will always remember how it felt to hug and be hugged by them, as well as my brothers and sisters. I felt tall next to my parents, even though I am only 4'10" myself, they were much shorter than I remembered.

Renata's husband, Little Heinz, managed to rent or borrow a larger car to take us around. We arrived at my parents' home and were made comfortable. It was a modest home. Under one roof, the living quarters were on one end, the barn and hay loft on the other end, with the milking room, bathroom, and papa's workshop in the middle.

Figure 20: My Beloved Papa & Mother, Karl & Selma

It was a bit of a culture shock for us at first. Not bad, just different. We were used to flushing toilets and hot running water, my parents' home had neither. It was outhouse-style toilet built inside the house, next to the milk room. The kitchen was simple and functional. Mother still cooked meals on an iron wood-burning cookstove. There was a large sink in one corner with a table that papa built for her;

it had a pull-out drawer that housed two deep metal bowls that she used for washing and rinsing dishes, or her hair. In the other corner was a small table under a window. They used cold storage in the basement to store milk and butter, they didn't have a refrigerator.

The living room had a tiled heating stove in the center that heated both their bedroom and the living room. There was a long table in the room with a small TV on top. Papa had figured out how to pick up channels from the west, so they saw programs like Bonanza and Lassie. He hid the antenna in the chimney so no one could see it. The living room held his favorite chair and a small china hutch. There wasn't much space in the living room while we were there because they brought in a big table where we could all eat together. Next to their bedroom, was the beautiful sunroom that papa built for mother's plants and winter herbs. Everything was easily accessible by a long hall that ran down the center of the shop and the house.

Upstairs were two bedrooms and stairs that led to an attic. The rooms were comfortable, each had an armoire and small wood stove to heat the room as well as water for bathing. Marvin and I were in the larger room, with a big bed for the two of us and a smaller one for Robbin. The other room had two single beds with a small table. We loved sleeping in those feather beds. If you haven't slept in a feather bed, you have missed a special experience; it surrounds you, engulfs you, hugs you. It's pretty amazing.

The kids would sit at the window in their long, narrow room. When you opened the door, you could smell the heavenly aroma of smoked meat that must have been stored there. At the top of the stair was a small room where papa set a wash tub; there was barely enough room to stand. After bathing, papa came up and somehow emptied the water out through the small window. There are so many memories and adventures that I could go on and on.

We had such a wonderful time and hated to see it come to an end. The family wouldn't let us spend any of our money while we were there because they thought we had spent enough just getting there. Finally, I was able to get Little Heinz to understand that we either had to spend the money or give it to the government when we left. It was our wish to use the money to buy my parents a refrigerator. My sister Erna worked in a store that sold appliances and just before we left we presented it to my parents. My mother was speechless. Then she turned to papa and said, "No Limburger cheese." We all laughed. Ironically, upon returning home we had to replace our refrigerator; our replacement was bigger and cost less money than the one we bought my parents.

Papa fought hard, using all his energy to get well so that he could spend quality time with us. He went on to live nearly twenty more years. It was heart breaking to leave, we had no idea if we would ever return.

After we left we reflected on our time there and the difference between cultures. We learned to converse even with a separation of two languages. Each of us came away with a different point of view. Marilyn summed it up well, "All people are a lot alike. They just want to live in peace and have a good life. Government is what causes most of the problems."

We returned to the West, reversing the route we came in, through no-mans-land again and arriving without incident in Hof. All of us breathed a sigh of relief. We spent a few days exploring Nuremberg and Erlangen where Marvin and I had been married. Erlangen is about 30 minutes north of Nuremberg and we were able to visit the church that we were married in.

Marvin, Robbin, and I made another trip to Germany in 1976 to celebrate my parent's 50th golden wedding anniversary. Even my youngest brother Adolf was able to join us. It was a very special time; we were a whole family, my parents and all of their six children.

Figure 21: Karl & Selma's 50th Wedding Anniversary, 1976

Marilyn and I were able to make a trip to Germany the very next year, 1977. We visited my parents and my brothers. It was wonderful to spend time with my best friend Vera. She met us at the train station in Bremen and joined us for the trip southwest to Trier to see Phil and his family who were stationed with the Air Force there.

Over the years, we traveled to Germany several more times.

Some family members were able to visit us in California as well. Renata's husband, Little Heinz, made his first trip to the west, out from behind the Iron Curtain, in 1988. Everything was a wonder to him. One day he devoted an entire eight-hours marveling at everything in Walmart. He loved Marvin's shop and would spend all day building things. Marvin and Little Heinz went many places together; it was a great experience for both of them. Renata and Little Heinz made several trips west, some together and some separately.

Jaentsdorf Survivor Reunion

Spring of 1988 brought some exciting news of a village reunion. I received word from Arthur Wallstein, the Burgermeister's son from my village of Jaentsdorf. They were planning a survivors' reunion. This would be the first survivors' reunion, or maybe it was the first one that I knew about. Several villages from my old province were doing this. The reunion would be held in Rothenburg on the Taube in Bavaria in the southern part of Germany. Unfortunately, I just couldn't see any way for me to get there.

My next-door neighbor, Joan Schumann, stopped by; we sat and talked as we often did. She listened to me tell about the letter, the reunion, and Germany in general. She and Al liked to travel. She enjoyed my stories of Germany, and especially of Bavaria.

The next morning Joan called. "If you had a way to get to the reunion, would you go?" Without hesitation, not really thinking about what she was asking, I replied, "Of course I would."

She was excited, she talked a mile a minute, "Then we need to get busy. You don't have much time. I have always wanted to go to Bavaria, to see the antiquity, the castles, the charm, everything. Al and I have never been there." I was still a bit stunned, not quite sure if I was really hearing what I was hearing. I don't know who was more excited, she or me. "You can be our interpreter. I have always wanted to see Germany. You don't want to miss that reunion. This would be a perfect fit." I was in a state of disbelief.

Before I knew it, we were off to my first village reunion and Joan's first trip to Germany. We would be gone for two weeks.

The reunion was wonderful. Over one hundred village survivors were there. Rothenburg was a wonderful place for the reunion, Joan was captivated by the well-preserved medieval old town. When we left Rothenburg, we headed north to a small town just outside of Wolfsburg to see some of modern Germany. We got a special tour of a huge Volkswagen plant. It was fascinating to see how the cars were made, this plant was building the Jetta. We toured a wind- and watermill museum. It was equally interesting to see all the different styles of mills, how they were powered by wind, water, or steam engines, and their many different uses.

A small group of us traveled together on the next portion of the trip. We stood on the streets of the town of Brome where a journalist was shot and killed back in the early 1960's by East German border patrol for nothing more than taking a picture of "The Wall". The Berlin Wall was literally built through the center of towns. Homes were cut in half and families torn apart by a division of the country by two different governments. People and their feelings didn't mean anything. I recall standing there with several others from the Jaentsdorf reunion staring at the high fence with guard towers on the other side, tears in our eyes from the senselessness of it all.

Over the course of the next few years I was able to attend at least six more reunions.

The very next year in 1989, Joan and I went back again, this time Marilyn accompanied us. We traveled together and also separately, while Joan stayed with some friends. We went into East Germany to visit my family. Marilyn noticed that something was very different, comparing this visit to our first one in the 1970. She said, "Look over there, the guards walking on patrol aren't even watching us. They seem so relaxed. Remember how unconcerned they seemed when we first came into no-mans-land this time? They even offered food and drinks for sale while we waited. The inspection was not nearly as long or hostile."

This was a loving but melancholy visit with my family. Mother had passed away in 1983 and Papa's spirit had never gotten over the loss. Watching us leave was also hard on him. Although we didn't know it at the time, this would be the last time I would see papa.

Who was to dream that within six months of our visit, on November 9th, 1989 the Berlin Wall came down. The separation of East and West Germany came to an end. We saw the differences as the country began to reunite. Many of my nieces and nephews took part in candle-light protests that led to The Wall coming down. Papa always said, "They cannot keep the good people of Germany apart" and he was right. Sadly, he did not get to see the Berlin Wall come down, he died shortly before it happened. Papa would have been proud of his grandsons and granddaughters for their part in the demonstrations.

1990 brought great change to Germany and over the course of the years to come. The East had to be rebuilt; much had been taken from them and what was there was old and falling apart. The economy hit a low, many had to look for work in other areas. Even today many of the cities that were booming before the war have become like ghost towns. Modernization did move in, slowly taking over.

Traveling into Berlin in 1990 in search of a telephone to make a call back to the United States we saw the progress with our own eyes. Phone cable was being placed everywhere, and many cities were getting the latest fiber-optic technology. The streets were torn up installing a new sewer system. We even saw a statue of Joseph Stalin that had been pulled over with his face in the rubble. We walked over two miles into West Berlin, walking through the Brandenburg Gate and what was left of the Berlin Wall. We did finally find a telephone to call home.

Each trip thereafter would find the two sides, East and West Germany, quickly becoming equal and then reunited as one. Today Germany is a great example of what can be accomplished when people are able to put their mind and resources to work together.

Closing Comments

The 21st century is something I never expected to see. I have celebrated many weddings and suffered the loss of many people I dearly loved. I have more grandchildren, great-grandchildren, and great-greats than I ever expected — five generations, and they are all "my kids". I worry about the successive generations and what kind of life they will have. I pray that they will not have to experience some of the hardships that I endured.

Nowadays my life has slowed down a bit. I spend less time doing for others and more time in my garden. I love to show everyone my garden. I don't drive much anymore and depend mostly on my kids for that. Each time I see one of their smiling faces, I feel blessed.

I hope I haven't bored you too much with my life story. At my age, I have seen the list of friends and family grow, as well as decline, sometimes all in the same year. Life is a mix of happiness and sadness. I've been through both. Losing your child before yourself is still the hardest, next to losing your spouse, and then close friends. Each has made me a stronger person, helped to shape me into who I am. I think I did ok.

I try not to hold anger toward those who have hurt me, and if I have, it is unknowingly. As I get older, sometimes I say things that don't seem to make sense, as I tend to mix old with new. If I repeat myself, please be patient; someday you may be doing the same thing.

These old eyes have seen many changes, things we take for granted now — from candles and oil lamps to lights that make night like day in every color imaginable. From horses to cars to planes and rockets. From artesian wells and outhouses, to hot running water and flushing toilets. From town talk and Red Cross posters, to radio, television, telephones, phonographs, videos, cell phones, the internet, and smart phones. From wood cook stoves to gas, electric, and microwave ovens. From wash buckets and clothes lines, to washing machines and dryers. There is so much more, it's mind boggling.

I could keep writing but somewhere the story must come to an end. So, let it be. God Bless you my children and dear friends. Thank you for all your love and support.

Before I close I do have one last thing I need to say. This is for all who have called me Mom or Grandma. Over the years there have been many who are family, even if they are not the same blood. Some are gone now. All who grew up with me and my children have become one large family. The chapters of my life could not be complete without each one of you in it.

Figure 228: In my garden, 2013

Hertha Hanna Kranz Bodle, Mom, Oma, grandma

.

EPILOG

Epilog 1: California

In 1963, we were starting over once more. We were now a family of eight, since Bill and Phil had families of their own. Selma was the oldest at sixteen and Robbin, the youngest at three. We had lived in Wyoming for seventeen years. It was the only home that our kids had ever known.

Marvin called from California and said, "Start packing. I'll be there next weekend to get you." It didn't take much for us to pack. We didn't have very much; we sold or gave away most of it. The following Saturday we loaded the kids and our belongings into the GMC truck and the station wagon. I think we must have looked like the Beverly Hillbillies. Bill came with us to help with the driving and to help us settle in. All of us were pretty excited, which made the long road trip easier.

We split the kids up between the two vehicles. We planned to take our time and enjoy some of the scenery on the way. It would be a three-day trip. We stopped inside Yellowstone National Park to watch Old Faithful and stretch at Fisherman's Bridge. We drove along the Madison River where we saw buffalo and elk. Somewhere inside the park we got caught in a big traffic jam caused by bear sightings. Johnny Cash's new song "Burning Ring of Fire" came on the radio. We heard it many times on that trip, learned the words, and would sing along with him.

The kid's excitement quickly wore thin. We drove at night so the kids would sleep most of the way. After we filled our thermoses with coffee, Marvin said that if I got tired, to just flash the headlights so we could all pull over. We didn't have walkie talkies, and cell phones hadn't been invented yet, so we had to work these things out in advance. I enjoyed listening to the music on the radio; now and then one of the kids would wake up to keep me company for a while. Selma would slide in behind me, I would slip to the other side; this is how we would relieve each other as we were driving along. When I think about it now, it sounds crazy. I also wondered how Marvin could drive all that way by himself and not get sleepy.

At dawn we pulled into a little truck stop in the middle of nowhere. Marvin said we weren't far from Reno, then we would be in California. We went into the restaurant to order breakfast. When the waitress asked little three-year-old Robbin what he wanted, he looked up at her with those big brown eyes and said, "I want a duck egg." The waitress looked completely surprised. She turned to us and quietly said, "I'm sorry, but we don't have duck eggs." Marvin grinned, "That's okay, just make them sunny side up. He will never know the difference." When she left with our order, we both snickered about it. After breakfast Robbin told the waitress that those were the best duck eggs ever. We had another giggle over it and got back on the road.

California's Central Valley was all farm land and orchards; it was beautiful. The valley where our new home was located was mainly orchards and farms separated by a few small towns. There were rows of trees, corn, tomatoes, or most anything you could want for the dinner table.

Marvin sent pictures and told us a lot about the house but hadn't quite told us everything. We pulled up to the house in a neighborhood that was probably built in the 1950s. Our house looked like every other house on the block, except it had a koi pond in front and a red front door. The previous owners had been Japanese and the yard was beautiful.

The red front door opened to the living room. The living room had a fireplace; we never had a fireplace before. Around the corner was the kitchen and dining room. Down the hall on the left was a bathroom and the master bedroom.

On the right were two more bedrooms. It was a small house, but it had everything we needed.

Out back there was a small strip of land and a fence. It contained a small fish pond and a gazebo. We were looking for the gate that led to the backyard. We looked at Marvin then back at the fence. He stood there with his hands in his pockets, "This is the best I could find. From the house to that fence is your backyard." What could we say?

The bedrooms were small but with bunk beds the kids would fit. The two girls took the smaller bedroom and the four boys would be in the larger room. Everything would be okay; I was sure of it. After the shock of the small house and yard, we busied ourselves unpacking. There really wasn't much to unpack.

New neighbors stopped by to greet us. The kids met other kids in the neighborhood. Our hunting friends came by, brought some food, and asked if there was anything else we might need. Before we knew it, we had a couch, dining table, and beds. It's amazing what people can come up with, stuff that is tucked away in their home or garage. At just the right moment, God answered our prayers. It was a great neighborhood filled with many wonderfully friendly and helpful people.

During the years in Campbell, all six kids graduated from high school and went on to find work.

From Scratching Out a Living to Supervisors

The first three years in California were difficult. Marvin was the sole breadwinner. He worked hard, working long hours, and we didn't have much money. He worked for a while doing maintenance work for a company that owned apartment complexes. After a slight downturn in the economy, Marvin lost his job to someone younger. That was really frustrating. Somehow, we managed to keep our heads above water.

We did whatever we had to do as a family to make it work. We took odd jobs and work when it came around; the whole family pitched in. Neighbors let us know of odd jobs: cleaning out places, hauling stuff to the dump, and tidying up properties.

By 1965 things were probably their worst. Money was tight. That summer I took the kids to Wyoming where we all helped in the fields for Bill's in-laws. This helped to pay for the expenses, with a little extra.

Marvin's father, Hugh, died on October 13th 1965; we made a special trip to Wyoming to be with family. We reconnected with Junior and his wife, Virginia. We saw each other quite a bit after that, Junior and Virginia lived in Salem, Oregon.

In November, Marilyn broke her arm. We did not have money to pay the medical bills so they reduced part of the cost and arranged for me to help care for an elderly lady. Within days, Marvin got word that Stanford Hospital on the Stanford University campus was looking for workers. He applied for the job and, as God would have it, we were all working before Christmas. Life began to look more promising.

Marvin worked for Stanford Hospital's facility engineering department. He started as just another carpenter and soon moved up, taking on more responsibility, moving from carpenter to foreman to head supervisor. Marvin worked at the Hoover Pavilion most of the time but also on the new Stanford University Medical Center. Stanford medical facilities are in a continual process of modernizing and expanding to accommodate new technology and new health care practices. Whenever there was change, Marvin's crew would be working on it. It was 1981, Marvin was 68 years old, and wanted to do some traveling with a friend in the trucking business. Marvin retired as Supervisor of the Carpentry Department after sixteen years. He had a great crew and they had a lot of respect for him.

Marvin joined Frank on the road. Frank Dalton Trucking delivered goods all over the U.S., as well as into Canada and Mexico. That was fun for a couple of months; then Marvin was ready to settle in to Pine Mountain Lake.

The elderly lady I worked with to settle the hospital bill passed away and I went to work for Pat Heath, helping her with her mother. I did this for several years until she too passed away. I was looking for other work, and a friend told me about a new company that was coming to Los Gatos, Becton-Dickinson.

The beautiful valley we lived in was rapidly changing. The large orchards of plums, cherries, apricots, apples, and oranges were disappearing, turning into industrial centers, subdivisions, and shopping centers. Blacktop and concrete replaced open fields and green trees. In the next decade, the area became known as Silicon Valley, for the many silicon chip innovators and manufacturers.

In 1966, Beckton-Dickinson was opening a new branch to make surgical gloves and tubing for stethoscopes. They were looking for people to fill all three shifts. I applied. The starting wage was $1.15 per hour for day shift, $1.25 for swing shift, and $1.50 for graveyard. I was surprised and excited to be hired for graveyard shift at such a good starting salary. The wage of $1.50 per hour doesn't sound like much, but I had no experience and if you compared it to 2018 dollars, it was the same as $11.55 per hour.

I started on the assembly line stripping gloves off a hot mold by hand. It was a never-ending production line. I looked down the row of molds shaped like hands, moving out of the dipping pot, in-and-out of the oven, and over to me in an endless line. It was sweltering in the room. We were called "strippers". Later a machine was brought in to do the stripping. We picked them up, inspected them, and boxed them off a moving assembly line. It was a great relief when they built a wall separating us from the heat of the ovens.

Marvin said, "You won't last a week." After all these years together, I couldn't believe he said that to me. Now, I was more determined than ever to prove him wrong. By the second week my thumb nails came off and my hands hurt. But, I wasn't going to complain or quit. I worked night shift for a year then moved to swing shift as a floor supervisor. I worked my way up, through all three shifts. When I made it to day shift, I moved into a lab technician position. I went to college to learn about formulas, data analysis, laboratory equipment, problem solving, and stuff like that. I retired from Beckton-Dickinson in 1981, after 15 years. Marvin knew I wasn't a quitter and I proved that to him once again.

Pine Mountain Lake

Today I live in a community called Pine Mountain Lake in the town of Groveland. It is in the Sierra Mountains close to Yosemite National Park. Marvin and I purchased the property in 1971, moving here full time in 1981.

It didn't take us long to fit in. We were busy with the new house, got to know a lot of neighbors, and got involved in the community. Marvin joined the local American Legion and VFW (Veterans of Foreign War).

I joined a small group of people that worked *FOR* the community. The idea formed one day, at an unlikely place, the dump. Roland Elliot and Ray Stevens went to the dump to dispose of their trash and spotted a perfectly good bag of clothes that had been tossed out. They both knew of struggling families in the area, families that had very little. Roland and Ray wanted to help.

I wanted to be a part of it too, so I asked how I could help. Soon, I had shoes to repair, buttons to sew, and zippers to replace on coats, shirts, and sweaters. Marvin made buckles for belts and shoes. It started out just as a gathering and grew into an organization of about twenty-five people. We called ourselves "Helping Hands". We were from all different walks of life with a wide variety of skills. It just started blossoming. I guess you could say that I was one of the original founding members but I more like to think I was just one of the helping hands.

Today Helping Hands is a wonderful network of volunteers and thrift shops for clothes, household goods, and furniture for people who care about value, who re-use, re-purpose, and recycle. It serves everyone with excellent merchandise, great finds, good deals, and bright smiles. I am proud to have been a part of starting Helping Hands and I continue to volunteer my time with them when I can.

Proud to Stand for my Principles

Life in Pine Mountain Lake was on a good roll in August 1987. We were busy and happy. We celebrated Marvin's birthday and our anniversary. It was a very hot, dry summer. We were happy when the clouds started to build, promising rain. We looked forward to the rain, but worried about lightning. Several smaller fires had already sparked at the higher elevations. One afternoon, about a week before Labor Day, we had a series of lightning strikes. Within days a huge fire started. At the time it was the third largest fire in California history; even today it ranks in the top twenty. The Stanislaus Complex Fire burned 145,980 acres and 28 structures.

The fire was very close to Groveland and we were on high alert. Our car was packed. We were ready to go if we got the evacuation notice. I was scared. Every time the big CalFire planes flew low over the house, memories of the Dresden bombing came rushing back to me.

We did evacuate and after what seemed like forever, we were allowed to return home. I was shocked at how close the fire had gotten to our house and the surrounding community. Marvin was speechless.

I heard that volunteers were needed to help serve meals for the fire fighters. I joined several other locals who returned and wanted to help. A company from Reno furnished the meals for the firefighting crews and welcomed our help. I got up at 2:00 in the morning to drive to the fire camp. We worked a nine-hour shift from 3:00am until noon, making and serving breakfast.

I volunteered throughout the entire operation, moving to three or four different locations over the course of a month. We served crews getting ready to head to the fire lines for the day as well as the returning crews. The returning fire crews were exhausted from the heat and smoke. We were so proud of them, it was a big job, we tried our best to cheer them up. Each day driving home we could see how bad it was and how hard they were working.

In the fall the town of Groveland threw a big thank you party for the firefighters and their families; even the Governor of California came, George Deukmejian. We called our thank you party "Thank God the Fire's Out".

Several women and some of the youth were asked to hostess the event. All the clubs donated workers and money. At the planning meeting I was asked to be one of the greeters for my volunteer role at the fire camp. One very tall lady got quite upset about this, remarking, "She is way too short and no one will see her. She should work in the kitchen instead." This hurt me deeply. Why should my size have anything to do with it? I told her, "Tall or short, fat or skinny, we are all human beings." I was given the position of greeter but her comment still bothered me.

On the big day of our thank you party I worked with my daughter Marilyn decorating the stage with plants and trees. With everything in order, I received my greeters' apron, went over to my stuff, pulled out "my hat", and put it on top of my head. Then I proudly walked out front to start my job as greeter.

My hat was an old Styrofoam hat that I decorated especially for the event. I took a piece of poster-board, cut out flames on the top, each flame listing one of the thirteen fires that merged to form the Stanislaus Complex Fire. In the center was a big thank you to the fire fighters. I glued the poster-board around the crown and side panels of the hat completely encircling it. When I put on that hat, I was taller than the woman who made the belittling comment.

As the firefighters arrived, it was me they spotted first and came over with big smiles and their questions. I greeted dignitaries and film crews, helping each find their seats and know the plans for the day. Quietly among the volunteers, many laughed with me as I proved my point — I may be small in stature, but I stand tall on principles.

A few weeks later, while I was picking up plants at the nursery the guy who was helping us kept saying that he knew me. I didn't recognize him. He then realized he had seen me on television the night after the thank you party. I didn't know it, but I made national news that night.

Figure 239: Complex Fire "Fire's Out" Celebration, 1987

Losing Loved Ones

Early in 1982, Marvin received a call from his brother, Junior. Life for Junior was unraveling and falling apart. Marvin drove down to Oceanside and moved Junior up to live with us, settling him into one of the upstairs bedrooms. We could tell that he wasn't feeling well but he never complained and helped around the house as much as he could.

In spring, I received word that my Aunt Emma, mother's sister and my Godmother, had passed away. In July, I received word that my brother Arnold's wife, Elfriede, had both legs amputated and lost her battle with diabetes.

Junior found work that summer on a sheep ranch down by Waterford; he really liked it. As fall set in, the weather turned cold, and we received a call from the rancher saying that we needed to come and get Junior. Junior had become quite ill and was not doing well at all, so we took him straight to the hospital in Modesto. They told us that he had lung cancer and it was advanced. Junior had always smoked a pipe, I can't remember a time when he didn't. When he came to live with us we didn't know how bad his health was and what little time we would have together. Junior passed from our lives a few days later in October of 1982.

We were now celebrating our second Thanksgiving and Christmas in our PML home. 1982 had been a difficult year; we lost family that we cared about, so 1983 came in with hope for of brighter days ahead. Life can, and will, take its own course and usually it is not what you planned.

Larry

On March 3rd we celebrated Larry's 27th birthday. Near the end of the month Marilyn and I returned to the Bay Area to attend a baby shower for one of Marilyn's girlfriends. It was Friday, so we left for home about 10:30pm, to avoid the traffic and to give Larry enough time to finish some work he was doing on Marilyn's Subaru Brat. Typical of this time of year, it was that unpredictable season between winter and summer.

Marilyn was driving. I was in the passenger seat beside her; four of Selma and Bud's kids were bedded down in the back sleeping for the drive home. We were chatting away, as the two of us always do. We talked about everything and how we enjoyed her girlfriend's baby shower that we had attended earlier in the day.

We were about halfway home when the Subaru started acting up. Marilyn pulled into an empty gas station under the lights, lifted the hood, and mumbled something about "not knowing anything about cars." She fiddled with a few things and somehow figured out that the air filter worked its way loose. Pushing it back down and locking it into place she said out loud, "I suppose Larry thinks I should become my OWN mechanic!"

We got back on the road, arriving home shortly before 2:00. We put the kids to bed and crawled off to bed ourselves. I hadn't yet fallen asleep when the phone rang. That was odd as it was the middle of the night. Marilyn answered it. A few moments later we heard her stumbling down the stairs. We knew something was not right. Bud was on the phone. His voice sounded strange, almost foreign as he told Marvin the news.

At 12:20 in the morning, Larry died in a freak explosion. He left for work early, ahead of two other boys, to get to the shop to do some welding, something the company allowed. The blast shook the area pretty hard. The two other boys said they saw and felt the explosion. When they arrived at the shop, there wasn't much left. They found Larry's body up against a wall. It was some type of gas explosion related to the welding equipment.

It was the hardest day of our lives. Losing a child. It wasn't right. A parent should always go first; that's the way it's supposed to be. To say it was difficult is an understatement. Marvin and I never really got over the tragedy. It's so hard to believe that a few hours earlier I hugged him and a short time later he was no more. I worried about the other two boys who I think blamed themselves. But thank God, they weren't there or all three would have been lost.

Work in my yard, along with Helping Hands, became my outlet or maybe my therapy after Larry's accident. About two months after losing Larry I got a call from the Red Cross telling me that my mother had passed away during the night. My father found her. He went to wake her, but she was already gone. Once more, my world was torn to pieces. I sat and cried for what seemed hours.

I had been working with Helping Hands for a big fundraising event in Groveland. Marvin insisted I go, even though I had just received the sad news of losing my mother. I reluctantly agreed. I got busy working, helping, and talking with all the people that came out. It was good. A German couple was in Groveland after visiting Yosemite Park and stopped to find out what all the activity was. Noticing that they were German, someone directed them to me. They were school teachers from Munich. We got talking and for some reason, it comforted me to speak my native language. I told them about losing my mother. Those two beautiful souls gave me comfort and peace that day when I really needed it, in a way that no one else could. It connected me with my homeland. God does work in mysterious ways. We just never know what a stranger may bring into our life.

In twelve short months I had lost five family members. Memorial weekend was our family celebration of life for Larry. For me it was a celebration of life for all five of my lost family members: Aunt Emma, Elfriede, Junior, Larry, and my mother.

We returned to Germany the next year. The time shared with each member of my family, especially my father, gave me a huge lift. Marvin and I visited Erlangen, where we were married. It was such a pleasure to be back. It is where our life together started. When we left Germany, we had seen so much, walked in history, and I was feeling renewed. I was able to gently close some chapters of my childhood by visiting family graves and saying my private goodbyes. I was so happy to make this wonderful trip with Marvin.

Losing Marvin

In December 1993 Marvin had a series of strokes from mild
to major. Marvin was a robust man with a strong will to live.
He pulled through working hard in rehabilitation learning to
walk and talk again.   Marvin was fitted with supplemental
oxygen after his strokes. He didn't always want to wear it,
complaining that it got in his way. He was often seen taking
off the breathing tubes, especially for photographs.

Figure 10: Marvin and me, 1994

In the fall of 1994 Marvin had a series of mini strokes. We
prepared to take him to the hospital. He could barely speak
but managed to say, "No more hospitals." Marvin was a

strong man and fought a tough battle with great dignity. He always helped and supported me as much as he could; I did everything I could to do the same for him. The whole family was with us for Thanksgiving.

By the beginning of December, Marvin steadily declined and Hospice increased the frequency of their visits. Our Hospice nurse spoke with the kids, explained what was happening and what to expect. She told them to talk with Marvin and let him know that it was okay for him to go and that they would be there to help me out. I think this was one of the hardest things our kids have ever had to do, giving their father permission to leave. By the day before Marvin left us, the entire family was at his side: Bill, Phil, Selma, Bud, Marilyn, Allen, and Robbin. Only Larry was missing, having lost him from our life eleven years earlier. Marvin left us Saturday morning, December 10th 1994, after eighty-one great years on this earth and forty-eight wonderful years of marriage. My life would never be the same.

Life is full but at a slower pace. I was honored to be made Grand Marshal for Groveland's 49er Festival in 2003. I work with Helping Hands when I am able. My garden brings me great joy.

Epilog 2: Family of Ten

Bill and Phil were four and three when we became a family. I always tried to view them as mine. There are probably some people who would say that was not the case, but in my mind and heart I feel that I did my very best. It was not easy for any of us.

The boys had a rough start in life. Maybe their mother, Deloris, wasn't quite ready to be a mother. It's hard to say what went on in her head. All I know is what others have told me and what little I saw with my own eyes. Deloris often left the boys alone with no one watching over them; she thought of herself, before the children. Other family members would step in to help, finding the little guys all by themselves with Deloris nowhere to be found.

Marvin and Deloris originally had three boys, Bill, Phil, and Bobby (William, Philip, and Robert). Bobby was the youngest. Marvin was in the Army, stationed in Europe, when the three boys were found left alone. Bobby got very sick and died before his first birthday. Bobby is buried in Clearmont, or maybe Sheridan. For Marvin, that was it. He divorced Deloris and got custody of the two boys. Divorce was uncommon in the 1940s. Usually, the mother got custody of the children. But, this was considered a case of abandonment and the court granted Marvin custody. Josephine and Hugh, Marvin's parents, cared for the boys while Marvin was in Europe with the Army.

I loved all my children, all eight of them. Over the years there were tears of joy and disappointment with each one. I know I may not have been a perfect mother, but then who *really* is? I know in my heart that before those two beautiful souls left me, I had done okay with them. I love and miss them dearly.

→ William Hugh Bodle was born in Sheridan, Wyoming on August 11th 1942 to Deloris and Marvin. Bill passed away in Texas on August 23rd 2009 from complications following heart surgery at the age of sixty-seven.

Most things came easy to Bill, especially in school, and likely with girls too. He was a tall, thin, handsome young man, much like his dad. As the years went by, many said he looked a lot like his Uncle Junior and Grandfather Hugh.

Bill and Phil were inseparable. We called them "the boys" because they did everything together. Where one went the other would follow. When they got into mischief I didn't always know who was the chief mischief-maker.

Bill worked in the energy industry, building expertise in geothermal and oil, setting up rigs for drilling. In later years, Bill and Phil teamed up, driving long-haul trucks across the U.S.

Bill married Scarlet Decker and blessed our lives with seven beautiful grandchildren, who have blessed me with eleven great-grandchildren, and eight great-great-grandchildren as I write this.

→ Philip Landen Bodle was born in Sheridan, Wyoming on November 12th 1943 to Deloris and Marvin. Phil passed away in Salt Lake, Utah on December 14th 2009, just four months after his brother Bill, from complications caused by cancer at the age of sixty-six.

Phil liked to see the results of his work. He loved fishing. Phil loved working with wood. He was an adventurous spirit. He didn't always take the best precautions and we often heard, "Hey! Look at me!" or "Watch this!" or "Look at what I'm doing!" just before some crazy stunt. That adventurous spirit included some pretty wild ideas and pranks.

Phil was career Air Force, joining right out of high school. He served in Korea and Vietnam. Phil was listed as M.I.A. (missing-in-action) for a year and a half. Many years after Phil retired from the Air Force, we learned that he was on a planned classified mission and not really M.I.A. at all.

Phil married his high school sweet heart, Bobby Joe Boyle in 1963. Phil and Bobby Joe blessed our lives with two beautiful grandchildren and one great-grandson. We lost Bobby Joe in 1998, when cancer returned after eleven years in remission. Phil remarried a short time later to Yvonne Hall.

➜ Selma Vera Sophie Bodle was born in Sheridan, Wyoming on May 1st 1947.

Selma reminded me of my mother and friend Sofie. I could always depend on her. Selma has never been much of a trouble maker. She somehow avoided the more mischievous things. She was a good big sister always helping with the younger kids.

Selma was a good worker and never without employment. She had several jobs over the years working with a medical supply distributor, Pacific Bell (the local telephone company), Hewlett Packard, and a couple of start-up companies that folded. After moving to Groveland she worked at the local hardware store.

Selma was married twice. First to James Cready blessing us with a handsome grandson in 1972 who later blessed us with a beautiful great-granddaughter. Next Selma married Robert (Bob) Watkins blessing us with a handsome grandson in 1977. Selma's husband, Bob passed away on April 2nd 2016.

→ Edwin Marvin "Bud" Bodle was born on August 1st 1948 in Sheridan, Wyoming.

Bud loved cowboy boots and cowboy hats from the time he started to walk; he would even wear them to bed, if we let him. He was often seen running around with nothing more than a diaper, his cowboy boots, and hat. The older Bud got, the more he reminded me of my own father. He is a blend of contrasts, sweet and sassy. Like my papa, Bud has a big heart and tries to please, but he is also a prankster. Bud can be outspoken and very blunt at times. I could hear papa in Bud's laughter and see him in the mannerisms.

Bud was a good worker and, like Selma, always seemed to have a job. Bud was drafted right out of high school and the Army sent him to Vietnam. He came back from Vietnam a changed man, more distant, only letting a few people get close to him. I wish that we would have talked more about our different experiences in that part of our lives. It may have helped us both better understand what we went through, better understanding each other too.

Bud married twice. First to Darlene Lombardy in 1971 blessing us with two grandchildren who in time blessed us with four great-grandchildren. Next Bud married Linda Pyse in 1996 bringing two (step) grandchildren into the family and adopting three other children, grandchildren to me. Linda passed away after fighting cancer.

→ Marilyn Carmon Bodle was born on June 9th 1952 in Powell, Wyoming.

Marilyn is artistic and free spirited. She can be strong-willed but can give in when needed. Sometimes she is giving to a point where she can be taken advantage of, a bit like her sister, Selma. Marilyn is strong and bold, not shy or withdrawn, yet she will tell you the opposite. We have traveled a lot together. She has been my rock since Marvin passed away. I look to her for guidance when I don't understand something. She has the same gentle ways as my mother — a good listener, patient, and kind. Similar to my mother, Marilyn uses plants to heal and does not care much for western medical practices.

Marilyn married John Robinson adding a (step) granddaughter to our family. John was not a good match for Marilyn, they split up, then she found the love of her life, Murray Smith in 1984. They have been together ever since. Murray added a (step) granddaughter. Between their children, five great-grandchildren have been added to our family.

Murray ran Down-to-Earth Construction and wanted to expand, in 1984 Murray brought Marilyn into the business opening a nursery and landscape supply. Later they opened up a hardware store in Big Oak Flat. Marilyn and Murray retired in 2013 selling the business.

➔ Allen Lee Bodle was born on July 28th 1953 in Powell, Wyoming.

Allen was always getting into, and out of things. He had a way of looking at me with those big dark blue eyes and a grin that was hard to resist. Allen loved to torment Marilyn. One minute they would be playing peacefully, the next minute pandemonium. Allen has an easygoing attitude, "if we can't get it done today, tomorrow we can work on it." Even so, he is determined to finish what he starts.

Allen would do whatever was needed to earn money. Like his brothers, Allen enjoyed working on cars, motorcycles, and anything with wheels. He liked the independence of driving trucks the best.

Allen married twice. First to Angie Ramos but it didn't last because he traveled so much. Later Allen married Bonny Ogilvie in 1996, figuring how to balance work and family.

Bonny brought two beautiful daughters with her (now granddaughters for me) adding five great-grandchildren.

→ Lawrence Ray Bodle was born on March 3rd 1956 in Powell, Wyoming. On Sunday, March 27th 1983 at the young age of twenty-seven Larry left us in an industrial accident.

Larry had a band of freckles that ran across his nose and big deep dimples that made his smile bigger than life. He was mischievous much like my papa. I got a taste of what my mother must have gone through. Larry could get into things so quick or disappear in a snap.

Larry was great with cars, trucks, and anything mechanical. By the time Larry was sixteen, he was working at the gas station down the street, just a few blocks away.

Larry had a special girlfriend, Joyce Reynolds, and they blessed us with a granddaughter and three grandchildren. Larry married Renee but they were not together very long before the accident and did not have any children together.

→ Robbin Karl Bodle was born on October 3rd 1959 in Powell, Wyoming.

This was the hardest of all my pregnancies. I started having problems mid-term. The doctor told me to stay off my feet as much as possible. Well, that was difficult, if not impossible, with a wild three-year old along with four other children at home ranging in ages up to thirteen. We also had Marvin's dad, Hugh, living with us at the time too.

We moved to California when Robbin was three years old, sadly he never had the homestead experience that the other kids had. After high school Robbin moved up to Groveland. He is quite a handyman and can fix just about anything. Robbin has done lots of different types of work over the years. He helped lay carpet, inventoried old car parts, assisted in construction, drove long haul trucks with his older brothers, worked as a plumber, and did some electrical work. There isn't much he can't do with his hands.

Robbin never married nor had any children. After Marvin passed away, I am very grateful that Robbin stayed in Groveland and lives with me.

APPENDIX

Appendix 1: Europe Map 1937 – 45

My childhood home was Jaentshdorf, Germany. Today this area belongs to Poland, in the Schlesien region. *Look for the dashed circle (right of center).*

To escape from Nazi Germany, I walked over 300 miles from Dresden to Graz, Austria (where we rested in relative safety), then onto Siegendorf, Austria to surrender. *Look for the solid circle (map center) for Dresden and solid line heading south to Graz, Austria (lower edge of map, just right of center) and then heading northwest to Siegendorf.*

Appendix 2: Poland's Schlesien Region – Home 1926-42

Map from a modern-day postcard of the Schlesien Region of Poland. Look for the star inside a dashed circle, this is the location of Jaentsdorf, my childhood home. Jaentsdorf is a short distance northeast of Breslau where I went to high school and began my medical training.

Appendix 3: Letter from Mother to Me, 1945

This is the last letter I received in Austria from my mother fleeing with my brothers and sisters, trying to stay ahead of the Russians, February 1945.

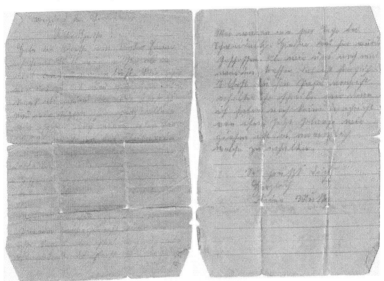

Appendix 4: Wyoming Map – Home 1947-62

Marvin was born in Montana and his family home was in Cody, Wyoming. Marvin and I lived in Wyoming for our first eighteen years together.

Yellowstone National Park, (not shown but located in the upper left corner of the state) was our favorite place. Yellowstone was the first National Park in the U.S.; best known for its wildlife and Old Faithful.

Sheridan (top, just right of center) was near our ranch. Bill, Phil, Selma and Bud were born in Sheridan.

Powell (top, just left of center) is closer to Yellowstone, and was near our homestead farm. Marilyn, Allen, Larry, and Robbin were born in Powell. The population of Powell was ~2,000 in 1945 and doubled to 4,000 by 1950 with the homesteading act.

Cody had a population of 3,000 in 1945, it's about 25 miles southwest of Powell. Named after William Frederick Cody, better known as Buffalo Bill, for his part in establishing the original town.

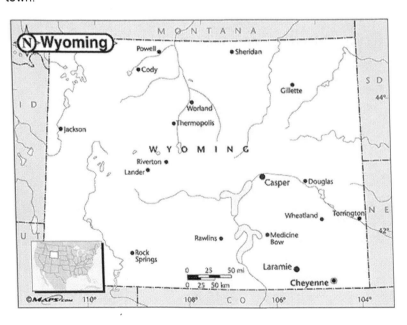

Appendix 5: Bay Area, California Map – Home 1963-81

Stanford University in Palo Alto is where Marvin worked for many years. *Look for a solid circle, lower center.*
Campbell is where our family home was from 1963 - 1981. *Look for the solid circle, lower right.*

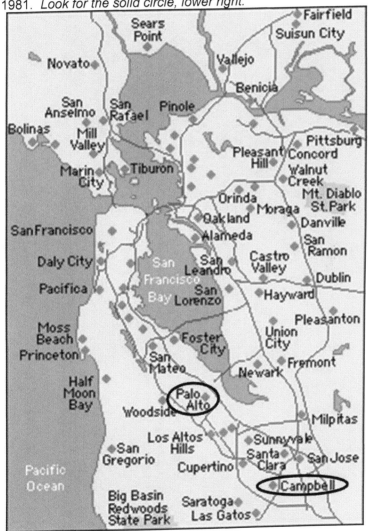

Appendix 6: Groveland, California Map – Home 1981

Groveland is where our family home is today. *You can see the town between the Hwy 49 and Hwy 120 signs.*
Yosemite National Park is one of our favorite places. *That's the darker shaded area to the west.*

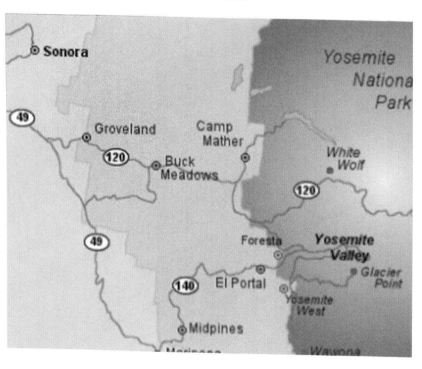

Appendix 7: A Forest of Family Trees

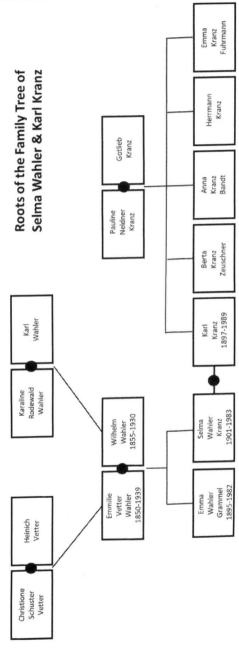

**Roots of the Family Tree of
Selma Wahler & Karl Kranz**

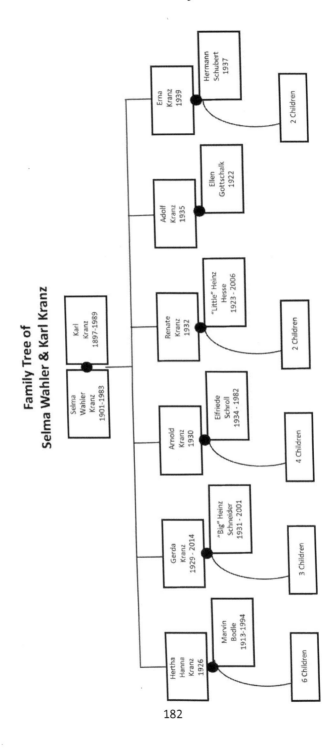

Family Tree of
Selma Wahler & Karl Kranz

Family Tree of Hertha Hanna Kranz & Marvin Bodle

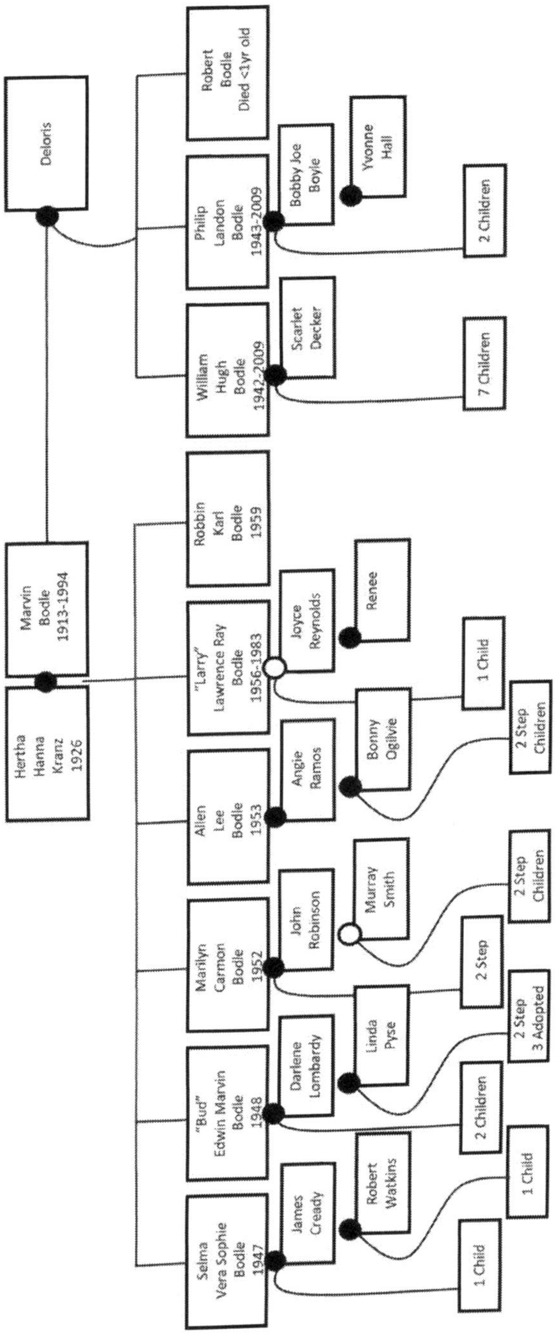

Appendix 8: Time Line

GERMANY - Jaentsdorf
1926 – Hertha Hanna Kranz, born March 29, 1926

1928 – Penicillin is discovered & sliced bread is invented

1939 – WW II Begins on September 1 (age 13)
1940 – Hanna attends High School in Breslau (age 14)

1942 – Penicillin is put into use to treat infections
1943 – Hanna is drafted into German Medical Corps (age 17)

1945 – Escaped during Dresden Bombing on February 13
    – WW II ends September 2
1946 – Marvin proposed March 29
    – Hanna and Marvin marry on August 24 & 25
    – Hanna leaves Bremerhaven for the US in November (age 20)

WYOMING – Powell Ranching
1947 – Selma Vera Sofie is born on May 1
    – Ranch Fire on September 8
1948 – Edwin Marvin "Bud" is born on August 1

WYOMING – Cody Homestead
1950 – Korean War begins

1952 – Marilyn Carmen is born on June 9
    – Hanna gets her first electric stove, oven, and refrigerator
1953 – Allen Lee is born on July 28
    – Korean War ends
1954 – Hanna is awarded U.S. citizenship on May 13
1955 – Drowning in oil, June 20
    – Vietnam War begins
1956 – Lawrence Ray "Larry" is born on March 3
1957 – First indoor bathroom on the homestead (age 31)

1959 – Robbin Karl is born on October 3
1960 – First automated household dishwasher is introduced (Miele)
1961 – Vietnam War escalates

– Berlin Wall is constructed

CALIFORNIA - Campbell
1963 – JFK is assassinated on November 22

1965 – Hanna sees Adolf, first family member in 20 years (age 39)
– Marvin begins work at Stanford University in November
1966 – Hanna begins work at Becton-Dickinson

1969 – Neil Armstrong walks on the moon, July 20
1970 – First trip back to Germany in 24 years, since 1946 (age 44)

1975 – Vietnam War ends on April 30
1976 – First complete Kurtz family reunion (age 50)

CALIFORNIA – Pine Mountain Lake, Groveland
1981 – Marvin and Hanna both retire

1983 – Lawrence Ray "Larry" dies on March 27 (he was 27)

1987 – Stanislaus Complex Fire

1989 – Belin Wall falls on November 9

1991 – Wide World Web went live (age 65)

1994 – Marvin Phillip dies on December 10 (he was 81)

2000 – Dot-com bubble bursts

2007 – iPhone is released (age 71)

2009 – William Hugh "Bill" dies August 23 (he was 67)
– Philip Landon "Phil" dies December 14 (he was 66)

2010 – iPad is released

2018 – Wrote her memoir (age 92)

Appendix 9: List of Images/Figures

Reading Group Questions

1. Hanna is forced to be independent from the age of 16. How do you think this shapes her?

2. What attracts Marvin to Hanna? What attracts Hanna to Marvin? In what ways do they complement each other? How would you describe Hanna and Marvin's relationship? Did their relationship change over time?

3. Hanna considered naming the book "Stand Tall", why would she have considered that as the title?

4. How would you feel leaving your native country for a land and a life unknown?

5. What did you like best about this book? What did you like least?

6. Hanna faced many difficult choices and decisions. What were they? What made them complicated and challenging? Did she have other options? If so, what were they? How would that have changed her life?

7. Did the book evoke any feelings of freedom and independence for you?

8. What gave Hanna a sense of purpose and fulfillment?

9. How would you compare life in Wyoming to Hanna's upbringing in Jaentsdorf? What are the similarities and differences?

10. Why did Marvin and Hanna leave Wyoming? What did they think they would find in California?

11. If your family was "lost" to you, how would that make you feel? Would that change the way you would act or react?

12. What places in the book would you like to visit? Why?

13. Why do you think Hanna chose to write this book?

14. What aspects of Hanna's story could you most relate to? What could you least relate to?

15. How honest do you think Hanna was being? Were there things that went untold? What do you think they were?

16. What gaps do you wish Hanna would fill in? Were there points where you thought she shared too much?

Made in the USA
Columbia, SC
13 November 2024

45999840R00119